# History of the
# Black Dollar

# History of the Black Dollar

Angel Rich

ISBN:1973939738
ISBN 13:9781973939733

# Special Thanks

**God**

Rica Rich (Mother) and Courtney Keen (Co-founder, The Wealth Factory)

Sharon Redmond (Aunt) and Brenda Sayles (God-mother)

Ms. Brenda A. White (Blow Elementary School), Ms. Josma (Kettering Middle School), Ms. Stephanie Loftin (Flowers High School), Dr. Freddye Davy (Hampton University), Dr. Sabin Duncan (Hampton University), Dr. Ruby Beale (Hampton University) and Dr. Sid Credle (Hampton University)

Sarah Thompson (VP, Global Market Research, Prudential), John Strangfeld (CEO, Prudential), Richard Carbone (CFO Prudential), Janis Bowdler (JP Morgan Chase), Maurita Coley (MMTC), and Dr. Maya Rockeymore (CPGS)

Congresswoman Maxine Waters, Congresswoman Eleanor Holmes Norton, Congressman GK Butterfield, Congressman Ron Dellums and Congressman Charles Rangel

Harry Wingo, Alexei Cowett, Rich Nelson, Mark Levine, Julia Spicer, Deb Tillet, Neil Davis, Steve Shapiro and Erin Horne McKinney

And a very special thanks to the Honorable Thomas Nida

# Foreword

*Advancing a 21ˢᵗ Century Wealth Equity Agenda*
Dr. Maya Rockeymoore, CEO, Center
for Global Policy Solutions

AFRICAN AMERICANS HAVE always worked hard for their dollars but their dollars have not always worked for them. From the earliest time on U.S. soil, there are examples of Blacks combining their ingenuity and labor to create innovative and lucrative businesses; managing to achieve financial success and social and political influence even during the darkest chapters in our nation's history.

Nevertheless, the story for the vast majority of African Americans has been one of economic marginalization and financial struggle. Released from slavery with nothing but the clothes on their backs and whatever skills they managed to accumulate on plantations, African Americans made the remarkable transition from being human capital to learning how to generate capital to support their families in a racialized system where they were too often met with maximum opposition to their success.

Despite surviving the indignities and horrors of the Jim Crow era and finally achieving voting rights, equal access to public accommodations, and broader educational opportunities during the Civil Rights era, many of the same systemic barriers that have historically plagued African Americans continue to be a factor today.

This circumstance is measured through what we refer to as the "racial wealth gap," the economic divide that leaves Blacks with a fraction of the wealth of Whites. Contrary to assumptions about African American spending patterns, researchers have shown that most of this gap can be explained by discriminatory policies, different educational and homeownership experiences, and labor market practices that too often leave Blacks with the short end of the economic stick.[1]

Depending on the data source, Whites are estimated to have about 10 to 17 times the median wealth of Blacks.[2]

When looked at on a dollar basis, the typical African American family only owns six cents for every dollar of wealth owned by the typical White family.[3] Given the history of Blacks in America, very few families are positioned to leave inheritances to their children.

This means that income—diverted into savings, investments, businesses, and other appreciating assets—should be the primary vehicle through which African Americans build wealth. Yet there is also a racial income gap with Blacks and Latinos earning only 67 cents for every dollar of earnings made by Whites. Given these disparities, it is not a surprise that the racial wealth gap exists at every income quintile. However, many people do not know that the racial wealth gap is largest at the lowest income quintile; with low-income African Americans possessing zero percent of the wealth of low-income Whites. Indeed, one study found that the average Black family would need 228 years to build the wealth of a White family in 2016.[4]

So where do we go from here? There is no doubt that African Americans should, to the extent possible, resist America's consumer culture that encourages

1 Tom Shapiro, Tatjana Meschede, and Sam Osoro. (2013). The Roots of the Widening Racial Wealth Gap: Explaining the Black-White Economic Divide. Boston, MA: Institute on Assets and Social Policy. Retrieved on April 23, 2017 at https://iasp.brandeis.edu/pdfs/Author/shapiro-thomas-m/racial-wealthgapbrief.pdf

2 Rakesh Kochhar, Richard Fry, and Paul Taylor. (2016). On Views of Race and Inequality, Blacks and Whites are Worlds Apart. Washington, DC: Pew Research Center. Retrieved on April 23, 2017 at http://www.pewsocialtrends.org/2011/07/26/wealth-gaps-rise-to-record-highs-between-whites-blacks-hispanics/

3 Rebecca Tippett, Avis Jones-DeWeever, Maya Rockeymoore, Darrick Hamilton, and William Darity. (2014). Beyond Broke: Why Closing the Racial Wealth Gap is a Priority for National Economic Security. Washington, DC: Center for Global Polic Solutions. Retrieved on April 23, 2017 at http://globalpolicysolutions.org/report/beyond-broke/

4 Chuck Collins, Dedrick Asante-Muhammed, Emmanuel Nieves, Josh Hoxie. (2016). The Ever-Growing Gap: Failing to Address the Status Quo Will Drive the Racial Wealth Divide for Centuries to Come. Washington, DC: Institute for Policy Studies. Retrieved on April 23, 2017 at: http://www.ips-dc.org/report-ever-growing-gap/

constant spending on frivolous items of little or depreciating value. African Americans should also take pains to avoid businesses and banks—such as payday lenders and banks offering exploitive loans with bad terms— that use wealth stripping business models to pad their bottom lines.

The biggest task ahead is launching and achieving a wealth equity policy and political agenda that pushes for systemic investments in K-12 financial literacy and capability, K-12 exposure to the principles and practice of entrepreneurship, post-secondary business accelerators targeting entrepreneurs of color and entrepreneurs of any race from low-income households, guaranteed access to business capital and supports, better opportunities for building matched savings over a lifetime (i.e. baby bonds, child savings accounts, portable retirement accounts, and Social Security), anti-wealth stripping laws that protect assets, and other opportunities for economic inclusion.

We also need to get our minds right. If used properly, the black dollar cannot only provide our families with generational wealth it can also accelerate the liberation of our communities. For this reason, I am proud of the knowledge and awareness that Angel Rich seeks to bring to African Americans through her seminal *History of the Black Dollar*. By uplifting African American stories as they relate to money and wealth, she is enlightening and inspiring a new generation of economic social justice warriors to take the helm in the fight to build a truly inclusive economy.

# Bartering Slaves (1619)

*Considered under law to be both person and property,
the slaves had no control over their lives as laborers*

THE SLAVE TRADE was an economic institution. Exporting and exploiting free labor from Africa directly contributed to the modern development of America, the Caribbean and Latin America as well as to the demise of Africa.

Legally, slavery allowed people to maintain "the right to purchase and own other human beings as property. These individuals were then able to profit from the labor of the people they owned who were forced to work without getting paid. Slavery, however, was not simply an institution that benefited propertied individuals; it was an economic system that allowed the United States, particularly the southern states, to develop as it did.

Slavery also hinged on the modern and pseudo-scientific concept of race, which is based on skin color. By constructing a belief of biological differences based on color, people who were called white justified the oppression of people who were called Black"[5]

Starting in 1619, slavery served as the nucleus for racial and economic injustice. This system prevented Blacks from receiving wages while providing high amounts of wealth to whites. While all whites did not own slaves, the socio-economic gains were massive and received by all whites. This division created the hotbed for the economic divide that still exist today.

Rich in agriculture, the South cultivated tobacco, rice, sugar, cotton, wheat, and hemp as the underpinnings of its economy. As the South became deeper,

---

5 Ending Slavery in the District of Columbia https://emancipation.dc.gov/page/ending-slavery-district-columbia

these industries became larger. Tobacco and hemp were staples in Virginia, Kentucky and Missouri while Maryland and Virginia focused on wheat. South Carolina and Georgia were prone to rice and sugar reigned in Louisiana. But throughout all the states, cotton stretched from the Carolinas to Texas. From the onset of the country through 1850, cotton was the most important crop to America.

Slaves managed large plantations doing everything from cooking, washing, sewing, blacksmithing, barrel making, sailing, horse training, growing crops and myriad of other activities. Each slave received one piece of clothing per year, usually some form of burlap. They received 1-2 meals per day depending on their master, usually grits.

Most slaves used food from the garden and sea to supplement the meals they were provided; creating Southern classic meals such as shrimp and grits. Collard greens were discovered by slaves attempting to find food deep in the woods. Slaves also used the garden to make home remedies for illnesses since doctors were only called for highly valued slaves.

The power and circulation of the Black dollar began in 1621. Shortly after slavery started a group of Black Virginians in 1621 earned enough money to purchase land where they formed a store selling tobacco and rice.

By 1700, Blacks started learning Native American languages which created more opportunities for them as trappers, scouts, traders and liaisons for whites. George Bonga from Duldo, Minnesota was a trader, trapper and interpreter at the signing of the Chippewa Treaty of 1837. James Beckwourth, a freed man and entrepreneur, helped Native Americans to discover a pass through the Sierra Nevada Mountains, named in his honor.

Another famous man named York, William Clark's slave served as the guide for the Lewis and Clark expedition. "His unique features and great strength were viewed with astonishment and awe by Native Americans encountered across the continent. His presence was considered a remarkable phenomenon that enhanced the prestige of the white strangers, who never had been seen previously by the isolated Indian populations."[6]

---

6  York, Lewis and Clark www.pbs.org

# History of the Black Dollar

Emanuel Bernoon and his wife Mary started another Black business of grave importance started in 1736. It's a little-known fact that this Black couple opened America's first oyster and ale house in Providence, Rhode Island.

In 1778, Richard Allen and Absalom Jones saw the budding economy of the Black community and formed the Free African Slave Society, the first organization to help educate newly freed people on socio economic issues.

Jean Baptiste Pointe DuSable, owner of a trading post, was also a trapper, farmer, and mechanic. He served as a middleman for Blacks, the British military, French settlers and Native Americans. He was the first to settle a little piece of land in Illinois – now known as Chicago. [7]

By 1800, Blacks owned several businesses but they were small-in-size and focused on the service industry. However, there were a few exceptions.

Mr. James Forten created a niche market for himself by becoming a master sail-maker who invented and patented a method for handling sails for sailboats. In 1832, he managed a full staff that included Blacks and whites in his Philadelphia plant, grossing $10,000. In 1846, Aaron Washworth became the largest cattle rancher in Jefferson County, Texas, owning 2,470 cattle and 4,578 acres of land.

Blacks were also among the first to master financial product sales in America. Thomy Lafon, real estate broker and business man, generated half a million dollars during his life. In fact, he left the money to several New Orleans charities including a Black school. Shortly after he died, Louisiana Legislature recognized him for his charitable contributions to New Orleans.

Despite these advancements, majority of Blacks remained in the harsh chains of slavery. During idle times, slaves would be leased to industrial employers and during even rougher times, or simply at will, would be sold. From "1805 to 1860 there was a well-established market for slaves, which meant that the slave was a highly liquid asset that could easily be converted to cash if the owners wished to sell the slave for any reason." Females were particularly valued for childbearing to increase their "stock."

"Considered under law to be both person and property, the slaves had no control over their lives as laborers. In 1860, approximately 400,000 whites

---

7  Chicagomag.com

owned 4 million slaves, equating to 12% of the white population controlling more than half of the slaves in the country, creating a power elite.[8]"

With this esteemed help, it's fascinating to know that the South still lagged the North by 20% in manufacturing. Wages for whites were lower in the South with per capita income at $103 compared to $141 in the North. The South was slow to develop due to a lack of reliable transportation, well-trained managers and modern technology.

# Willie Lynch (1712)

"Gentlemen.

I greet you here on the bank of the James River in the year of our Lord one thousand seven hundred and twelve. First, I shall thank you, the gentlemen of the Colony of Virginia, for bringing me here. I am here to help you solve some of your problems with slaves. Your invitation reached me on my modest plantation in the West Indies, where I have experimented with some of the newest, and still the oldest, methods for control of slaves. Ancient Rome would envy us if my program is implemented. As our boat sailed south on the James River, named for our illustrious King, whose version of the Bible we cherish, I saw enough to know that your problem is not unique. While Rome used cords of wood as crosses for standing human bodies along its highways in great numbers, you are here using the tree and the rope on occasions.

I caught the whiff of a dead slave hanging from a tree, a couple miles back. You are not only losing valuable stock by hangings, you are having uprisings, slaves are running away, your crops are sometimes left in the fields too long for maximum profit, you suffer occasional fires, your animals are killed. Gentlemen, you know what your problems are; I do not need to elaborate. I am not here to enumerate your problems, I am here to introduce you to a method of solving them.

In my bag here, I have a full proof method for controlling your black slaves. I guarantee every one of you that, if installed correctly, it will control the slaves

8 Economic Impact of Slavery http://www.encyclopedia.com/humanities/applied-and-social-sciences-magazines/economic-impact-slavery-south

for at least 300 hundred years. My method is simple. Any member of your family or your overseer can use it. I have outlined a number of differences among the slaves; and I take these differences and make them bigger. I use fear, distrust, and envy for control purposes. These methods have worked on my modest plantation in the West Indies and it will work throughout the South.

Take this simple little list of differences and think about them. On top of my list is "AGE," but it's there only because it starts with an "a." The second is "COLOR" or shade. There is intelligence, size, sex, sizes of plantations, status on plantations and attitude of owners, whether the slaves live in the valley, on a hill, East, West, North, South, have fine hair, course hair, or is tall or short. Now that you have a list of differences, I shall give you an outline of action, but before that, I shall assure you that distrust is stronger than trust and envy stronger than adulation, respect or admiration.

The Black slaves after receiving this indoctrination shall carry on and will become self-refueling and self-generating for hundreds of years, maybe thousands. Don't forget, you must pitch the old black male vs. the young black male, and the young black male against the old black male. You must use the dark skin slaves vs. the light skin slaves, and the light skin slaves vs. the dark skin slaves. You must use the female vs. the male, and the male vs. the female. You must also have white servants and overseers [who] distrust all Blacks.

But it is necessary that your slaves trust and depend on us. They must love, respect, and trust only us. Gentlemen, these kits are your keys to control. Use them. Have your wives and children use them, never miss an opportunity. If used intensely for one year, the slaves themselves will remain perpetually distrustful.

Thank you, gentlemen."

# King Cotton (1793)

*The enslavement of millions of slaves helped*
*Europe to acquire the capital*
*needed to finance the Industrial Revolution*

— ERIC WILLIAMS

IN 1754, THE number of slaves peaked at 250,000. At that time, the number of slaves in America were beginning to dwindle, a result of the Revolutionary war with many believing that slavery was coming to an end. Tobacco lands were beginning to deteriorate and southern crop prices were declining. In 1789, the US Congress was established and in 1794, George Washington called southern slaves "a very troublesome species of property."

However, technology intervened.

Eli Whitney patented the cotton gin in 1793. Eli's father "had solved the critical problem of removing seeds from cotton by developing a kind of comb to do the job. Whitney's cotton gin simply mechanized this comb.⁹"

Suddenly, with profits on the horizon, the slave population jumped from a quarter-million to four million. The demand for cotton from the North and Europe skyrocketed as the South had the best and cheapest cotton in the world. The slave economy then shifted from the upper South (Maryland and Virginia) to the lower South.

While the slave trade was abolished in 1808, expansion of slavery continued into the lower South from the domestic slave trade of the upper South.

The South experienced its' first major, nationally publicized uprising in 1822 in Charleston, South Carolina. After being suppressed by the city, Demark

9  Black Inventors Before the Civil War http://www.uh.edu/engines/epi127.htm

Vesey, a free minister, planned an insurrection. However, the plan was exposed two months before the riot was to take place. Vesey was trialed and hung along with 36 co-planners. Charleston firmly displayed their punishment throughout the country to discourage any future for uprising.

By 1830s, "cotton was king" and more than half of all US exports consisted of slave-grown cotton. In fact, slaves grew 60% of the world's cotton – thus paying for a substantial amount of iron and manufactured goods that led to more American growth.

The increase of labor needed to grow and manage the cotton exasperated the slave population and worsened their treatment. This tension led to the most famous slave rebellion in the history of America, led by Nat Turner.

A Black slave in Southampton, VA, Nat received a vision from God to free the slaves. He started by uniting his friends, killing his masters, and moving on to kill all the slave owners in his surrounding neighborhood. His movement quickly grew in numbers and violence. His soldiers, as he referred to them, killed more than 50 white men, women and children. The results of his rebellion are still felt throughout the veins of America today. Whites were terrified; increasing the amount of random arrests and attacks of Blacks out of fear.

By 1850, 1.8 million of the 2.5 million slaves were on cotton plantations, primarily as field hands. Commercial crops produced by slaves required a host of middlemen. The North focused on a myriad of businesses that supported cotton production in the South such as textile factories, insurance companies, shippers and cotton brokers.

The irony is not missed that Eli Whitney was himself a Black slave – known on paper as a white man named Sam. Plenty of slaves created inventions and new technologies, but they were not allowed to patent it. In 1858, the US Attorney General ruled that since slaves were property, their ideas, including patents, were also the property of their masters. For this reason, many Blacks – slaves or free – would file patents in their lawyer's name to improve their chances of acceptance.

There was also another slave, Jefferson Davis, who created a new screw propeller for steam-driven ships. Naturally, it was not patented but it did help the South's progress in the war.

Henry Blair became the first freedman to receive a patent in 1834 for a new seed-planter.

The cotton plantation economy was part of the much larger local, national and international political economy. The financial, shipping and manufacturing industries were all dependent on slave-produced cotton. Given that cotton ran the United States, and the US was competing for leadership in the global political economy, it is inarguable that slaves were the foundation of the US economy.

Banks would provide seed investment to purchase land and slaves. Slaves were literally viewed as a form of property – a commodity that could easily be sold and converted into cash. Individually and collectively, they were often traded as collateral for goods, services and a multitude of business transactions[10].

Slaveholders leveraged their slaves as shares of investments, using them to secure loans and pay off debt. Sometimes entire families would get destroyed from slaveholders placing bets they couldn't cover and would pay with a slave instead. When assessing estate values, the value of the slaves would be included. Taxes were even paid on slave transactions, providing a tax revenue source for local and state governments.

Basically, the United States turned slavery into political capital, leveraging cotton. Taking it a step further, the US Constitution incorporated the "three-fifths compromise" that allowed the South to count their slaves as three-fifths of a person when calculating the states' representation in Congress. This shifted the balance of power from the North to the South.

"It is inconceivable that European colonists could have settled and developed North and South America and the Caribbean without slave labor. Moreover, slave labor did produce the major consumer goods that were the basis of world trade during the eighteenth and early nineteenth centuries: coffee, cotton, rum, sugar, and tobacco.[11]"

In 1944, Eric Williams published a book titled *Capitalism and Slavery* where he depicted slavery as the growth engine of Europe's global economy. In it he

---

10  How Slavery Helped Build a World Economy http://news.nationalgeographic.com/news/2003/01/0131_030203_jubilee2_2.html

11  Was slavery the engine of American economic growth? https://www.gilderlehrman.org/history-by-era/slavery-and-anti-slavery/resources/was-slavery-engine-american-economic-growth

states that the enslavement of millions of slaves helped Europe to acquire the capital needed to finance the Industrial Revolution. Thus, Europe and America's progress was paid for at the expense of Black slaves who built the foundation for modern capitalism.

Interestingly, it would be this same need for economic self-interest and preservation, not ethical obligation, that would cause the North to fight for the end of slavery nearly 300 years after its start.

# Paul Cuffee (1759 – 1817)
Slave Activist, Explorer, Pioneer

Born on Cuttyhunk Island in Massachusetts on January 17, 1759, Paul Cuffee was one of 10 children of a freed slave and a farmer. In 1766, his father purchased a 116-acre farm in Dartmouth, MA on Buzzard's Bay. Upon his death, he left the farm to Paul and his brother John.

Leveraging his inheritance, Paul "bought and built ships, developing his own maritime enterprise that involved trading the length of the US Atlantic coast, with trips to the Caribbean and Europe."[12]

By 1780 he had become highly active in political affairs. Along with his brother and five other Black men, he filed a petition to protest free Blacks not having a right to vote in the election. Interestingly, he was arrested but his taxes got reduced.

Paul felt that free Blacks "could establish a prosperous colony in Africa." He dreamed of sending at least one ship full of Blacks to Sierra Leone every year with the ship returning with African goods to be sold.

Great Britain erected a settlement in Sierra Leone for London's Committee of the Black Poor. In 1787, it was named the Province of Freedom. Many of the Blacks that heavily populated Sierra Leone had found escape in the Revolutionary War via the British Black Loyalists.

---

12 Who Led the First Back-to-Africa Effort http://www.pbs.org/wnet/african-americans-many-rivers-to-cross/history/who-led-the-1st-back-to-africa-effort/

Later, in 1792, Freetown was founded when the Black Loyalists arrived from Nova Scotia. This group included George Washington's former slave, Harry Washington. Sierra Leone officially became a colony in 1808.

To disarm the Brits and Americans that were in favor of slavery as he pushed his agenda forward to colonize Africa, Paul founded the Friendly Society of Sierra Leone in 1811 to help "Black settlers of Sierra Leone, and the natives of Africa generally, in the cultivation of their soil, by the sale of their produce.

The following year, he visited Baltimore, Philadelphia and New York to establish American versions of the British' Committee of the Black Poor. Paul named his organization the African Institution. "It had self-contained branches in each city, and was charged with mounting a coordinated, Black-directed emigration movement."[13]

James Forten, the wealthy sailmaker and inventor, was Paul's close friend. He was the Secretary of the Philadelphia African Institution and Prince Sunders, a teacher and Secretary of the African Masonic Lodge, was the Secretary of the Boston African Institution. It quickly picked up momentum amongst the Northern Black thought leaders.

In 1807, America established an embargo on British goods and was battling weakening relations with Great Britain. On April 19, 1812 in Westport, MA, Paul's ship was seized by US Customs upon his return from Sierra Leone and Great Britain. He was charged with violating the embargo and the US denied the release of his cargo. At that point, Paul appealed directly to President James Madison.

On May 2, 1812, Paul Cuffee became the first Black man to sit down in The White House with the President himself and Albert Gallatin, Secretary of Treasury.

After pleasant exchanges and a great conversation about building a Black colony in Africa, the President ordered the release of Paul's property.

In an historic exertion, Paul Cuffee sent 28 Blacks (including 20 children) to Sierra Leone on December 10, 1815; spending $5,000. Upon their arrival on February 3, 1816, the explorers became the first Blacks to voluntarily return to Africa through a Black initiative.

---

13  Who led the first Back-to-Africa Effort http://www.pbs.org/wnet/african-americans-many-rivers-to-cross/history/who-led-the-1st-back-to-africa-effort/

Sadly, Paul's dream of building a great nation in Africa began to dissipate. In a letter to Paul Cuffee dated January 25, 1817, James Forten depicts a large meeting of Blacks at Richard Allen's Bethel AME Church. He said "three thousand at least attended, and there was not one soul that was in favor of going to Africa. They think that the slaveholders want to get rid of them so as to make their property more secure."

Doubling down on his perspective, Forten co-authored a statement later that year in August saying "the plan of colonizing is not asked for by us. We renounce and disclaim any connection with it."

Possibly from heartache, Paul Cuffee died one month later on September 7, 1817; killing "the dream of a Black led emigration movement."[14] The movement would later be picked up by the likes of Marcus Garvey, Henry Garnet, and others.

# Gil Sage Salvo Perkins
Words Liive Founder

Sage Salvo, born Gilbert Newman Perkins, is an artist- entrepreneur, Halcyon Incubator Fellow, and Economics PhD candidate. Sage has presented at the SXSWedu Conference (South by Southwest) in Austin, Texas, the TEDx MidAtlantic Conference in Washington, D.C., the DC Education Festival, and was a Keynote speaker at the IB (International Baccalaureate) Americas Conference this past July.

Sage is the Founder and President of Words Liive, LLC and father of CGI, Contemporary Grammar Integration. Words Liive is an educational program based on an original grammar transformation algorithm that Sage developed and obtained an international provisional patent on. The literary algorithm is a language evaluation and teaching process called CGI. The Words Liive program features algorithms and games that increase students' reading and writing proficiency over classroom texts including novels, poems, plays, short stories,

---

14  Who led the first Back-to-Africa Effort http://www.pbs.org/wnet/african-americans-many-rivers-to-cross/history/who-led-the-1st-back-to-africa-effort/

and other literary texts all via the medium of popular urban music, social media text, and computer programming language!

Sage has developed partnerships with Teach For America, City Year, College Success Foundation, Guerilla Arts, and COSEBOC. He is a 2011 MBA graduate from the University of Toronto and has also received two distinct Bachelor Degrees in Accounting and Finance from the University of North Carolina at Charlotte, in 2003 and 2004 respectively. The Washington D.C. native is a registered member of The American Society of Composers, Authors, and Publishers (ASCAP) and actively serves on several panels, radio show features, and programs concerned with education, technology, music, and culture.

# Black Codes (1821)

*"Constitution "knows no distinction of color. That all who are not slaves are equally free...equally citizens of the United States"*

— WILLIAM COSTIN

BECOMING THE NATION'S capital in 1791, DC was formed from land the federal government provided Maryland and Virginia; two slave states of the Chesapeake. In 1800, Blacks comprised 25% of DC's population at 14,093; majority slaves.

As the demand in the nation's capital grew, Blacks were forced to construct the US Capitol, the White House and other historic buildings. Major DC ports, Georgetown and Alexandria (until 1846) became major hubs for the slave trade. Today, DC has one of the largest Black populations in the country and Alexandria is the owner of America's largest housing authority.

Some DC slaves earned small wages and would save their money to buy their freedom. Others would gain freedom through the death of their masters. Reproducing for decades, the free Black population started to expand.

Pro-slavery whites, including the mayor, Robert Brent, began to grow concerned – so they introduced Black Codes. This was an effort to "solidify slavery as an institution and to strengthen the concept of racial segregation in the city. They also restricted the meaning and practice of legal freedom for free Blacks."[15]

In 1808, the mayor and alderman set forth the first set of Black Codes. With these laws in place, it became illegal for "Negroes or loose, idle, disorderly persons" to be outside after 10pm. If caught, Blacks would be imposed

---

15 Ending Slavery in the District of Columbia https://emancipation.dc.gov/page/ending-slavery-district-columbia

a fine of $5 (equivalent to $75 today). Those that did not pay the fines would be whipped. These rules were light compared with the stricter set of Black Codes introduced in 1812. Fines increased to $20 for curfew violations and free Blacks did not pay would be jailed for 6 months – entering the convict leasing programs. Slaves would be jailed and whipped with 40 lashes for nonpayment. Furthermore, freedmen were required to carry their freedom papers always.

Not to be out done, Mayor Smallwood kicked it up a notch in 1821 with a new set of Black codes. It required Blacks to "appear before the mayor with documents signed by three white people vouching for their good character, proving their free status. They also had to pay a peace bond of $20 to a respected white man as a commitment to good behavior. This code illustrates the precarious nature of freedom for non-enslaved African Americans, by attempting to control the movement of people of color."[16]

Famous freedmen such as William Costin, refused to pay the peace bond. He argued that the Constitution "knows no distinction of color. That all who are not slaves are equally free…equally citizens of the United States."

Interestingly, the judge that presided over his case ruled that while the Black codes were legal, they could not be enforced on freedmen who were residents before the codes existed. While small in nature, it was a huge achievement for Black America. Taking his victory further, Costin then contended that the concept of race was ill formed as his ancestors were respectively Cherokee, European, and African. Who was to define him as just African-American?

Starting in the late 1820s, groups began to organize to petition Congress for the abolition of slavery in DC.

There were more free Blacks than slaves by 1830 in Washington, DC. Thousands of petitions from slaves, churches, schools, societies and businesses would make it through the House of Representatives doors throughout the decade leading southern Congressmen to establish the Gag Rule in 1836. This rule banned the introduction of any bills or petitions about slavery.

This rule was also the result of the Snow Riot of 1835 with newspapers reporting that DC had its own Nat Turner. The paper stated that the 18-year

---

16 Ending Slavery in the District of Columbia https://emancipation.dc.gov/page/ending-slavery-district-columbia

old slave, Arthur Bowen, attempted to kill Anna Maria Thornton, the wealthy widow of William Thornton, Architect of the US Capitol.

Mrs. Thornton owned Arthur and his mother at her home on F Street NW. An angry mob of Irish mechanics gathered at Judiciary Square to demand the hanging of Arthur Bowen.

They were also upset with local abolitionists who were fighting to end slavery in DC. Pointing their attention to Dr. Reuben Crandall of Georgetown, they mob had the police search his residence for anti-slavery materials. Upon discovering various publications, he was charged with incitement to rebellion. The mob then demanded the hanging of Bowen and Crandall – together.

Being prevented by the police to reach either individual, the mob then set their sights on Mr. Beverly Snow's Epicurean Eating House on 6th Street and Pennsylvania Ave NW. Destroying the restaurants furniture and inventory, Snow was forced to leave DC. The mob looted everything from Snow's restaurant and then continued to destroy other Black-owned businesses. Among them were some of the first Negro churches and schools in DC; owned by Reverend John F. Cook on 14th and H streets, NW. Rev. Cook too fled DC, landing in Pennsylvania. This riot was the most symbolic display of anti-slavery in DC at the time.

The most famous and interesting slave revolt in DC was the Pearl Incident of 1848. 77 of the prettiest slaves, mostly women and children, from Georgetown and Alexandria attempted to escape on a 64-foot cargo.

Chartered by two white men, Daniel Drayton and Captain Edward Sayres, the ship was growing a reputation for bringing slaves to freedom for a fee. The Captain withstood the heavy risks because he needed the money.

Daniel Bell, a free blacksmith working in Navy Yard, was told he needed just $100 to help his family escape DC. While they were legally free, lawyers had tied them up in court. Paying the fee would be a much cheaper option and easier route to freedom. Bell joined together with other Blacks, including President Madison's slave Paul Jennings and Samuel Edmonson who wanted to help free his enslaved sisters, Emily and Mary. They were notoriously known throughout DC for their beauty and were prized slaves.

During the celebration of the new French Republic while DC was filled with activity, the ship waited for the slaves at the wharf on the Potomac River in Southwest, DC. They planned to reach the Chesapeake Bay and then sail to Pennsylvania.

Since the ship could hold more than the Bell and Edmonson families, others asked to join the exciting crusade, reaching 77 passengers. The ship allowed anyone to board that could get on by midnight.

Gathering in small groups on a dark Saturday night, the Pearl set sail down the Potomac River to head to Alexandria, VA. The next day, 41 white families woke up to find their slaves gone and quickly formed a group to find them. Sponsored by the Justice of the Peace and others, 35 armed white men went franticly searched DC, MD and VA for the slaves by land.[17]

After searching all over for them by land, the slave owners received a tip of their whereabouts -from a slave! This particular slave had a crush on one of the Edmonson sisters and did not wish for them to leave. In a very cryptic phrase, he hinted to the slave owners that the group had escaped by water not horses as they previously assumed.

With this news, the slave owners boarded the steamboat Salem and traveled 100 miles to overtake the Pearl at Point Lookout where weather had forced the freedom ship to dock. The escape provided pro-slavery supporters with ammunition to attack abolitionist for three days. Both captains were arrested and a group of slave-owners demanded they be hung.

Most of the captured slaves were sold to the deep south of New Orleans and Georgia. It is rumored in DC some of the prettier slaves were not sold or whipped due to their beauty, but rather just forced to walk a long distance as part of their punishment. A small select few gained their freedom through this initiative.

While unsuccessful, the Pearl Incident was America's largest escape attempt and raised national attention for the abolition of slavery and the slave trade.

Shortly after this incident, Congress voted to return the portion of DC that had been provided by Virginia in 1846. This forced all Blacks living in that portion to immediately lose any protection they had from DC, especially for education. All Blacks schools closed immediately in that part of town and

---

17 The Escape on the Pearl Schooner https://zinnedproject.org/2013/04/the-escape-on-the-pearl-schooner/

remained closed for 15 years until the Union Army entered Alexandria during the Civil War. [18]

The following year, an established white abolitionist, Gamaliel Bailey, became editor of the anti-slavery newspaper, The National Era. This paper was founded by the American and Foreign Anti-Slavery Society and focused on ending the slave trade in DC. It is noted as being the original publisher of Harriet Beecher Stowe's famous novel, *Uncle Tom's Cabin*.

With tension boiling over, the Compromise of 1850 was introduced to "appease both sides by ending or preventing the introduction of slavery and the slave trade in new states while allowing slavery and the slave trade to continue in states where already legal." This resulted in "the introduction of a slave-trade act that prevented the importation of enslaved people into the District for resale or transportation elsewhere, but continued to allow the sale of enslaved District residents to slave holders."[19] The images of slaves walking through DC handcuffed after being sold or being sent off for convict leasing did not leave the city. It was a precarious time for DC as the free slaves then outnumbered slaves by two to one. To be exact, there were 8,461 freedmen and 4,694 slaves according to the US Census of 1850. The Compromise of 1850 and the repeal of the Gag Rule in 1844 grew national attention as momentum for abolitionists; sparking the demand for Congress to exercise its constitutional power to end slavery.

Serving as the headquarters for numerous Union forces, Black refugees, soldiers and sailors began flocking to DC. "Refugee camps were created to accommodate the new residents, often near the sites of forts that are preserved throughout the District. There were camps at Duff Green's Row on First Street between East Capitol and A Streets SE, at Camp Barker at 12th Street and Vermont Avenue NW, and at Freedmen's Village in Arlington, VA." [20]

On April 23, 1861, after the attack on Ft. Sumter, Jacob Dodson wrote a letter to the Secretary of War to say, "I have some three hundred reliable

---

18 Ending Slavery in the District of Columbia https://emancipation.dc.gov/page/ending-slavery-district-columbia

19 Ending Slavery in the District of Columbia https://emancipation.dc.gov/page/ending-slavery-district-columbia

20 Ending Slavery in the District of Columbia https://emancipation.dc.gov/page/ending-slavery-district-columbia

colored free citizens of this City, who desire to enter the services for the defense of the City." The reply he received stated that "this Department has no intention at present to call into service of Government any colored soldiers."[21]

In December 1861, Henry Wilson of Massachusetts, entered a bill to end slavery in DC. Amazingly, the bill passed and was signed into legislation on April 16, 1862. Congress then added an addendum on July 12, 1862 to allow slaves whose owners had not filed for compensation to do so and allow Blacks to testify about their claims. That same week, Congress passed the Second Confiscation and Militia Act, freeing slaves nationwide whose owners served in the Confederate Army.

# Nat Turner (1800 – 1831)
Prophet

Nat Turner was born on the Virginian plantation of Benjamin Turner, who allowed him to learn to read, write and study religion. He was sold three times during his childhood and hired out to John Travis in the 1820s. He grew to become an intense preacher in his Southampton County neighborhood, saying that he was selected by God to free the slaves.

Turner was a heavy believer in signs and divine voices. During his childhood when Nat was three or four years old, he told some children about an event that happened before he was born. After his mother questioned him about his story, she confirmed its truth and was astonished at his ability. She felt he would surely be a prophet and was intended for a great purpose.

Nat was always a natural leader amongst his friends. They counted on his superior judgement as they felt he had Divine inspiration. Once it was largely discovered that Nat was going to be something great, he "studiously avoided mixing in society, and wrapped himself in mystery, devoting his time to fasting and prayer."

"Seek ye the kingdom of Heaven and all things shall be added unto you" was his favorite passage and he prayed daily for clarity on it." One day, while Nat was

---

21 Ending Slavery in the District of Columbia https://emancipation.dc.gov/page/ending-slavery-district-columbia

praying, the spirit spoke to him saying "Seed ye the kingdom of Heaven and all things shall be added unto you." For two years Nat prayed constantly for even more clarity. Finally, he had the same revelation, confirming to himself that he was ordained for a greater purpose with God. He then grew stronger in God, hardening his belief on ending slavery.[22]

Understanding the amount of trust his fellow slaves had for him, Nat began to prepare them for his purpose by informing them something was about to occur that would fulfill the great promise made to him. Around this time, Nat was placed with an overseer that he ran away from only to return after thirty days of hiding in the woods. The other slaves were surprised to see him, having thought that he had escaped to some other part of the country as his father had previously done.

He says he returned because the spirit appeared to him and said that he had his wishes focused on this world and not Heaven so he should return to the service of his earthly master – "For he who knoweth his Master's will, and doeth it not, shall be beaten with many stripes, and thus have I chastened you."

Nat then had a vision – he saw white spirits and black spirits in battle, and the sun was darkened, the thunder rolled in Heaven, blood flowed in streams and a voice rung out saying "such is your luck, such you are called to see, and let it come rough or smooth, you must surely bare it." This caused him to sink deeper into reclusiveness for the avowed purpose of serving the Spirit entirely. His vision revealed to him the knowledge of the elements, the revolution of the planets, the operation of tides and changes of the seasons.

He then received the true knowledge of faith as the Holy Ghost came to him saying "Behold me as I stand in the Heavens" and he looked up to see the forms of men in different attitudes – and there were lights in the sky to which the children of darkness gave other names than what they really were – for they were the lights of the Savior's hands, stretched forth from east to west, even as they were extended on the cross on Calvary for the redemption of sinners[23]."

Nat was puzzled by these great miracles and consistently prayed the meaning of them to be made certain to him. Shortly afterwards, while in the field,

---

22  http://www.melanet.com/nat/nat.html
23  http://www.melanet.com/nat/nat.html

Nat found some corn with drops of blood on it as though it were dew from heaven. After sharing his story with white and Black neighbors, he found hieroglyphic characters and numbers with the forms of men in different attitudes portrayed in blood on leaves in the woods, representing the figures he'd seen before in the Heavens.

At that moment, it became clear to him that the Holy Ghost was revealing itself to him, helping him to understand the miracles that had been shown to him. The message was: "For as the blood of Christ had been shed on this earth, and had ascended to heaven for the salvation of sinners, and was now returning to earth again in the form of dew – and as the leaves on the trees bore impression of the figures I had seen in the heavens, it was plain to me that the Savior was about to lay down the yoke he had borne for the sins of men, and the great day of judgment was at hand." [24]

He shared this vision with a white man, whom stopped his wickedness and was attacked with a cutaneous eruption, resulting with blood oozing from his skin. After praying and fasting for nine days, the man was healed. The Spirit then appeared to Nat again, and said "as the Savior had been baptized so should we be also." [25]

With this message, the slaves attempted to get baptized but the white people would not allow them to be baptized by the church so they went down into the water together before their family and friends who were also baptized by the spirit.

On May 12, 1828 Nat heard a loud noise in the heavens and the Spirit instantly appeared to him saying "the Serpent was loosened and Christ had laid down the yoke he had borne for the sins of men" and that Nat should fight the Serpent because "the time was fast approaching when the first should be last and the last should be first."

Nat then determined that Heavenly signs would help him to know when to strike. He felt it was important to keep his plans to himself until he witnessed the first sign.

---

24   http://www.melanet.com/nat/nat.html

25   http://www.melanet.com/nat/nat.html

# History of the Black Dollar

When the sign came to him – an eclipse of the sun – in February he decided to prepare to take the lives of the sinister people that enslaved him with their own tools of evil. Gunfire! Upon receiving the sign Nat told his closest friends about his plan and the messages he received – Henry, Hark, Nelson and Sam.

After much deliberation amongst themselves on how best to execute their plot, they landed on 4th of July as the day they would commence their attack. However, the foursome continued to debate so much over their plans that Nat fell ill in the process and the time passed without a final decision. When the sign appeared to Nat again, he knew he could wait no longer.

On August 21st, more of Nat's friends joined the movement as Henry, Hark and himself cooked dinner for Sam, Nelson, Will and Jack in the woods. Nat welcomed them and greeted them as they arrived. When he asked Will why he joined the group he replied that "his life was worth no more than others, and his liberty as dear to him." This made Nat fully trust Will thereafter.

They stayed at the feast until about two hours in the night until they went to the house to find another friend, Austin, who they all went to the cider press to drink with except for Nat.

Although Nat described his master as kind, feeling that the master had great confidence in him, the group was definite that they wanted to start at their own big house led by Mr. J. Travis. The group spared no one, regardless of age or sex and armed themselves with equipment along the way. Approaching the house, Hark went to the door with an axe to break it open. Although they knew they were strong enough to overpower the family if they were disturbed by the noise, the crew decided to kill them in their sleep so they didn't alert the neighbors.

Hark retrieved a ladder and placed it against the chimney. Nat then climbed up the ladder, entered through a window, came down stairs, unlocked the door and removed all their guns. With a hatchet in hand and Will at his side, Nat entered his Master Travis' chambers in the dark. Not easily killed on the first strike, Travis leaped from his bed and yelled for his wife. It was his last word. Will killed the slaveholder with a swift blow of his axe, following up with a double serving to his wife while she still lay in bed.

Five in total laid slain in their sleep when the gentlemen left. Awhile after they left, they remembered that they forgot about the infant that was asleep in the cradle. Returning to kill it, they took the opportunity to also gather four guns, some old muskets and a pound or so of gun powder.

Celebrating, the crew went to a barn where Nat organized them as soldiers and taught them all the maneuvers he had learned. He then marched them off to Mr. Francis' house, about 600 yards away.

Sam and Will were the first to approach the door and knock. When Mr. Francis came to the door, Sam told him he had a letter for him to get him to open the door. Once inside, the pair grabbed him, dragged him out of the door and repeatedly beat him in the head. He was the only white person in the family.

From there the justice seekers set off for Mrs. Reese. Proudly, they remained in stealth silence as they marched to her home where they discovered the doors unlocked. Entering with ease, they killed Mrs. Reese while sleeping in her bed. Alerted by the noise, her son yelled out "who is that" as his last words.

Happily, the crew then headed for Mrs. Turner's property about a mile away from Mrs. Reese's house. They reached the estate around sunrise, on Monday morning. As they approached the property, Sam, Austin and Henry went to the still. Austin found and killed Mr. Peeples there while the others went into the house. The family saw them coming and quickly shut the door. With a stroke of his axe, Will opened the door back up; finding Mrs. Turner and Mrs. Newsome in the middle of a room, scared to death. Will immediately killed Mrs. Turner. Nat took the sword he had when he was apprehended and struck Mrs. Newsome several times in the head but was unable to kill her because the sword was dull. Upon discovery of this difficulty, Will killed her as well.

As like all the other times, the crew then ransacked the house in search of money and ammunition. By this time, Nat's crew numbered 15. Nine of the men were mounted on horses and started for Mrs. Whitehead's property while the other six headed to Mr. Bryant's.

As they approached the house Mr. Whitehead was discovered standing in the cotton patch. The group called him closer to them. As he came nearer, Will, the executioner, sent him to an early grave. They then pushed forward to the house. Upon entering, Nat saw a girl running around the garden and chased after her. Once he finally caught up to her he realized that the girl was a servant and set her free. Once he got back to the house, the family had been murdered except for Mrs. Whitehead and her daughter Margaret.

As expected, Will "nearly severed her head from her body with his broad axe." Concealed in a corner of the cellar cap now stood Miss Margaret. Running from Nat, she was soon engulfed with repeat hits of his sword and a final blow to the head with a fence rail.

Returning from their duties, the other six came back with good news of the murder of Mr. Bryant. They then split again to go to Mr. Porter's and from there Mr. Francis'; the others to Mr. Harris' and Mr. Doyles' homes.

By the time they reached Mr. Porter, he had already safely escaped with his family. At that moment, Nat realized that the alarm of had been sounded and that word of his unrest was starting to spread. He left immediately to retrieve the others that had been separated from them, killing Mr. Doyle on the road along the way.

On his way to Capt. Harris' he checked the homes of Mr. Edwards and Mr. Barrow for his company, but found the whites were already killed. He found most of the crew at Harris', amped and ready to start their next round; the men now numbered at roughly forty, rejoiced in jubilation as Nat Turner rode up the yard, loading their guns and drinking. Meanwhile, Capt. Harris and his family had escaped so they destroyed the property in the house, taking his money and valuables.

Nat then ordered them all to march to Mr. Waller's, two or three miles away from their location at 9am, Monday morning. Stationed at the rear, Nat saw it his place to "carry terror and devastation" wherever they traveled. He situated 15-20 of his best soldiers in the front. These gentlemen usually entered the houses as fast as their horses would allow; serving two purposes – prevent escape and strike fear in the residents. As such, Nat usually entered the houses with the murders committed before he could reach the door. Nat recounts that sometimes he would get a sight of the murder in action and he would watch in silent satisfaction, immediately desiring his next victim.

After Mrs. Waller and her ten children were killed, the take-no-prisoners team set their sights on Mr. Williams. In the midst of killing him and his two kids, his wife escaped and got pretty far from the house. However, she was captured and bought back to the house where she was showed the mangled body of her dead husband. She was then told to lay by his side where she was shot dead.

Killing a few more families and gathering more soldiers, they now stood fifty or sixty in total, all mounted and armed. Nat decided to head for Jerusalem, VA as soon as possible.

On their way there, they reached Mr. James Parker's gate and many of the infantry wanted to kill his family for personal reasons. Trying to explain to the group that Parker had already left for Jerusalem, Nat remained at the gate on the road with eight others about a half mile away from the house. After waiting a while for them, Nat grew uneasy and headed towards the house after them. On their return, they were met by a group of white men led by Capt. Peete who had tracked their blood-stained path, firing at them on site, splitting up the group. Nat was not aware this was occurring as he had not been rejoined by the group just yet. Upon discovering this, he told his men to stop and face them.

There were 18 white men standing about 100 yards away from them when one of them prematurely fired. Taking advantage of the situation, Nat and team blitzed them with firing rounds, killing most of them. To Nat's surprise the white men had a second location about 200 yards away that they ran right into while chasing the first set of whites. The hill at the second location served as a rest stop for the other whites to gather and reload their guns. This party knew that Negroes were in the field and they tied their horses up to wait for them to return to the road, knowing that Parker's family was in Jerusalem.

On hearing the firing with Capt. Peete the whites immediately rushed to the area just in time to arrest Nat's infantry and save the lives of their fellow slaveholders. The whites began reloading their guns with more coming than was there originally. Many of Nat's bravest men were wounded, making the others panic and escape across the field. With the white men chasing them, Hark's horse was shot from underneath him. Nat miraculously caught another one for him as it was running by him.

Realizing that he had been defeated at that point in time, Nat planned "to go through a private way, and cross the Nottoway River at the Cypress Bridge, three miles below Jerusalem, and attack that place from the rear." He anticipated that they would look for him on the other road and he badly wanted to retrieve more guns.

After walking a little bit with roughly 20 of his soldiers he decided to return to go back to look for his lost soldiers that he was sure had walked back to their old neighborhoods. He figured he could convince them to rejoin him, bring new friends and head to Jerusalem with him.

Unable to find any more victims, they stopped at Major Ridley's quarters. Being joined by four of his men and new recruits, they were now 40 strong again. Nat decided to finally get some rest but was soon awakened by a loud noise. Nat was informed that they were about to be attacked and hopped on his horse. As he began to give orders his loyal crusaders followed his instructions while the newcomers ran. He was then back down to 20.

Turner managed to hide nearby for six weeks until his discovery and hanging in Jerusalem, Virginia alongside 16 of his followers. The riot struck fear in the heart of Southerners, ending the emancipation movement in that region, forcing harsher laws against slaves and deepened tensions between slave and non-slave holders.[26]

# Trevor Brooks
Founder, GunBail

*Taking guns off the streets*

Trevor Brooks was in and out of the prison system throughout his young adult years in Baltimore City. Growing up in inner city neighborhoods, it wasn't hard for him or his friends to get their hands on guns. Brooks was convicted of his first gun crime as a teenager.

Trevor Brooks founded GunBail to get guns off city streets and help non-violent inmates "I grew up in a culture of violence in Baltimore City, and as I got older, I wanted to do something to and positively impact my community, to

---

26  http://www.history.com/topics/black-history/nat-turner

do something that made a difference for minority young adults like me," Brooks said.

That's how the idea for his startup GunBail came about. GunBail's concept would allow family or friends of arrested individuals to exchange firearms for prison bail. Brooks, 46, is hoping to launch a pilot for the company, in partnership with law enforcement in Baltimore City, early next year.

Here's how it works: If someone is arrested for a nonviolent offense and it's determined by law enforcement that they could be eligible for GunBail, their family and friends will be notified. They can then download the GunBail app and follow the process to surrender a gun. They take a picture of the gun so it can be identified. Then GunBail provides a secure shipment box. Once the gun is secured, GunBail can track and retrieve the box. The gun is delivered directly to law enforcement, no questions asked, and processed in exchange for an inmate's release.

The mission is two-fold, Brooks said. It helps get illegal firearms off the streets and allows nonviolent offenders, who otherwise may not be able to afford it, gain access to bail.

Brooks realized the potential for the idea when he started researching gun proliferation and found about 75 percent of arrested individuals can't afford bail release and over 50 percent have some access to an illegal firearm.

"I saw that intersection as an opportunity to make a difference," Brooks said. "There are all these people who are arrested for nonviolent offenses. And they have access to illegal guns, but can't afford bail. So I thought 'What if I created a conduit for them to safely surrender their guns in exchange for bail?'"

GunBail's service comes with a fee of $99 per transaction. That's opposed to what could be a multi-thousand dollar bail payment. At the same time, Brooks says it costs the Baltimore prison system about $73-$132 per day to house an inmate.

Brooks said he is in the process of raising his first funding round, with a goal of $800,000. He said he is also in talks with eight other municipalities about introducing the service.

"The good thing is, we've seen a lot of interest and not one person or city we're marketing to has told us 'No,'" Brooks said. "Proliferation of guns is a huge societal problem and we've found a way to make a difference."

*Extracted from Baltimore City Biz*

# Civil War (1861)

*"All we knew was that the first colored troops sent*
*South from Massachusetts only got seven dollars a*
*month, while the white regiment got fifteen."*

— HARRIET TUBMAN

THE CIVIL WAR between the North and the South began on April 19, 1861. Black soldiers did not receive equal treatment to white soldiers in any fashion. The Militia Act of 1862 was the first official act encouraging and allowing Blacks to enlist in the Union Army. This law was "intended to let former slaves become laborers for Union army forces occupying the South but instead created regiments of Black soldiers." [27] Blacks were not officially authorized to engage in combat until the Emancipation Proclamation.

Blacks were integral to the success of the Civil War. Their roles consisted of being soldiers, nurses, laborers, spies, and doctors. More than 180,000 Blacks served in the Civil War in a regiment known as the United States Colored Troops.

181 Black nurses served in military hospitals in DC, Maryland, Virginia and North Carolina during the war with Harriet Tubman at the helm. Tubman helped innovate the nursing industry and implemented cleaning practices to reduce diseases. She served in multiple military hospitals before being heavily requested to take over the Colored Hospital at Fort Monroe Virginia in 1865 — the beginning of the nursing school at Hampton University.

---

27 African American Soldiers Protested Their Low Pay http://civilwarsaga.com/african-american-soldiers-protested-their-low-pay/

Some Black men were army surgeons "but they were confined to military hospitals or recruiting stations because white surgeons refused to work along-side them in the field."

Disguising themselves as slaves or laborers, Blacks also served as spies to view military documents. The information they collected was referred to by the CIA as "Black dispatches." Tubman along with Mary Elizabeth Bowser, John Scobell and Mary Touvestre were spies.

Most people do not realize that some Blacks joined the Confederacy as laborers, cooks and caretakers. Roughly 10,000 Black men served as soldiers and 50,000 as laborers for the Confederacy. While their motivation is unknown, researchers believe they may have been forced by their masters.

"Despite their loyalty and sacrifice, African American soldiers in the Union army were not paid as well as white soldiers." [28]

Harriet Tubman, who was a major leader of the Black Militia, was disgusted upon learning how much less they were receiving - 63 cents for every dollar whites made. In some cases, whites received $13 a month while Black soldiers received $10 a month minus $3 for their clothes, leaving them with $7.

Harriet Tubman decided to protest her pay and the other Blacks joined with her. They refused to accept any compensation until it was equal to whites. Corporal James Henry Gooding wrote a letter to Lincoln asking for equal pay:

"Now the main question is. Are we Soldiers, or are we LABOURERS. We are fully armed, and equipped, have done all the various Duties, pertaining to a Soldiers life, have conducted ourselves, to the complete satisfaction of General Officers, who, were if any, prejudiced against us, but who now accord us all the encouragement, and honour due us...have dyed the ground with blood, in defense of the Union, and Democracy...We have done a Soldiers Duty. Why can't we have a Soldiers pay?"

Sgt. William Walker of South Carolina and his fellow soldiers went on strike in November of 1863. Threatened with mutiny, most of the soldiers returned

---

28  African Americans in the Civil War http://civilwarsaga.com/african-americans-in-the-civil-war/

to work. Sgt. Walker refused and by February was convicted and executed by a firing squad.

The tension over equal pay turned Harriet Tubman against Lincoln and she refused to meet him out of protest. When asked if she ever met Lincoln, Tubman responded:

*"No, I'm sorry now, but I didn't like Lincoln in them days. I used to go see Missus Lincoln, but I never wanted to see him. You see we colored people didn't under-stand then he was our friend. All we knew was that the first colored troops sent South from Massachusetts only got seven dollars a month, while the white regi-ment got fifteen. We didn't like that. But now I know all about it and I is sorry I didn't go see Master Lincoln."*

She later grew to admire him after Sojourner Truth "told her Lincoln was not an enemy but a friend to African Americans."[29] Sojourner leveraged her reputation to become one of the heaviest recruiters for Black troops in the Union Army.

In June of 1864, Congress passed a law enforcing equal pay. The pay was retroactive for 18 months for most soldiers and men that were free before the Civil War. Interestingly, many troop leaders would allow soldiers to take the Quaker Oath to get around these stipulations. The oath is declared by God's law, not man's law, they "owed no man unrequited labor on or before the 19th day of April 1861."[30]

The protests continued without the Black soldiers accepting pay until March of 1865 when Congress finally awarded retroactive pay back to their enlistment dates. Still not satisfied with the amount not being equivalent to whites, Harriet Tubman continued to refuse her pay. She was nearly 90 years old before she ac-cepted compensation from the military.

Battlefields were extremely hazardous for Black soldiers. Those captured by the Confederates were sold into slavery and most often than not, slaughtered.

---

29 Harriet Tubman Didn't Like Lincoln http://civilwarsaga.com/harriet-tubman-didnt-like-abraham-lincoln/

30 African American Soldiers Protested Their Low Pay http://civilwarsaga.com/african-american-soldiers-protested-their-low-pay/

During the Fort Pillow Massacre, hundreds of Black troops were killed after the battle ended.

These incidents inspired new laws such as the Lieber Code of 1863 that protected Black soldiers from being sold into slavery and the Emancipation Proclamation, leading to the 13$^{th}$ Amendment.

By the Civil War, the South's per capita wealth could not be matched by Italy, Spain, Mexico or India until nearly 100 years later. The slave industry was still growing and thriving late into the 1850s. Nevertheless, slavery opponents began to argue that it was prohibiting true economic growth. "Despite clear evidence that slavery was profitable, abolitionists – and many others – felt strongly that slavery degraded labor, inhibited urbanization and mechanization, thwarted industrialization, and stifled progress, and associated slavery with economic backwardness, inefficiency, indebtedness, and economic and social stagnation."

The North was ready to end slavery not because it hated racism but rather because they "viewed slavery as an intolerable obstacle to innovation, moral improvement, fair labor, and commercial and economic growth."[31]

# Sojourner Truth (1797 – 1883)
Civil and Women's Rights Activist

Born in 1797 as Isabella Baumfree, Sojourner Truth was one of 12 children from James and Elizabeth Baumfree in Ulster County, New York. At 9 years old, with her family being split apart, Sojourner was sold at an auction with a flock of sheep for $100.

Sojourner recalls her new owner as brash and violent. She was then sold two more times, finally landing with John Dumont at West Park, New York.

Sojourner fell in love with a slave named Robert in 1815 and they had two daughters. Upon finding out, Robert's owner forbade the relationship because the children became the property of Sojourner's owner and did not benefit him.

---

31 Was slavery the engine of American economic growth? https://www.gilderlehrman.org/history-by-era/slavery-and-anti-slavery/resources/was-slavery-engine-american-economic-growth

As a result, in 1817, Dumont forced Sojourner to marry another, older slave named Thomas. They had a son and two daughters.

The State of New York started discussion on abolishing slavery in 1799 and then emancipated all slaves on July 4, 1827. This impacted Sojourner differently than others as she had just escaped to freedom with her infant daughter one year before the emancipation after Dumont reneged on his promise to free her.

At the time, her other children remained behind. Sojourner learned that her son, Peter, had been sold illegally to Alabama. Taking the issue to court, she won and had her son returned from the South. This was one of the first court cases in history where a Black woman successfully challenged a white man. After his rescue, Peter remained with her until he took a job on a whaling ship called the Zone of Nantucket in 1839. Sojourner received three letters from him between 1840 and 1841, but when his ship returned to port in 1842, Peter was not on it. She never heard from him again.

In 1843, Isabella Baumfree changed her name to Sojourner Truth, devoting her life to being an abolitionist. In 1844, she joined Northampton Association of Education and Industry, an organization founded by abolitionists to support over-all reform, especially for women. The members lived together on 500 acres of a self-sufficient community that encountered visits from William Lloyd Garrison, Frederick Douglass, David Ruggles and more. The community ended in 1846.

*The Narrative of Sojourner Truth: A Northern Slave* was published as her memoirs in 1850. During that same year, Sojourner was a key speaker at the first National Women's Rights Convention in Worcester, Massachusetts, kicking off her tour around the country. She, along with Frederick and Harriet had become celebrities as slaves turned abolitionist leaders.

Perfecting her speaking talent, Sojourner delivered Ain't I a Woman? in 1851 at the Ohio Women's Rights Convention in Akron, Ohio. Interestingly, when the first version of the speech was published it did not include the question Aint I a woman? This phrase did not appear until 12 years later in a Southern printed version. Researchers suggest that it is unlikely for Sojourner to have used such broken English since her first language was Dutch.

Her fight for political equality was radical for its time. She criticized the abolitionist community for placing such a heavy emphasis on civil rights for men, and felt women should be equally promoted. She argued that the heavy focus on men would ultimately leave Black and white women still struggling for women's rights.

On November 26, 1863, Sojourner Truth died at her home in Battle Creek, Michigan. Along with her family, she is buried at Battle Creek's Oak Hill Cemetery. She is remembered as one of the pioneers of the women's rights and abolition movement. She left her footprint on prison reform, property rights and universal suffrage. In 1920, nearly four decades after her death, the Constitutional Amendment barring suffrage discrimination based on sex was ratified.[32]

# Carita Marrow
Sr. Relationship Manager, United Negro College Fund

*Advocating for women and civil rights in Science, Technology, Engineering and Math*

Serving as Senior Manager at UNCF, Carita manages the Science Education Initiatives. Her focus centers on the Fund II Foundation UNCF STEM Scholars Program, a $48 million initiative designed to provide scholarships and support for 500 African American High school students who aspire to earn STEM degrees and pursue STEM careers. Acting in this role includes recruiting scholar's candidates, managing a selecting, on-boarding the students for a face-to face orientation and administering scholarships in addition to providing academic support services. In addition, Carita serves as program manager for the host committee for the HBCU Innovation, Commercialization and Entrepreneurship Initiative (HBCU I.C.E.), one of the Five Private-Sector Initiatives launched at the First White House Tech Inclusion Summit in February 2013.

Under this initiative, each year, UNCF brings a group of talented computer science students and faculty from Historically Black Colleges and Universities (HBCUs) to Silicon Valley for a four-day summit. Carita co-organizes these UNCF HBCU Innovation Summits. The four-day summit empowers students of color to chart their career paths within the STEM fields and establish a

32 Sojourner Truth Biography http://www.biography.com/people/sojourner-truth-9511284

presence in Silicon Valley. UNCF HBCU Innovation scholars have interned or have full time roles at the likes of Google, Adobe, Pandora, and Apple. Carita's role includes building strategic partnerships with technical companies and entities such as Google, United States Patent Office, VISA, Adobe, Salesforce, Yelp, Square, eBay, White House Initiatives HBCUs, etc.

The faculty initiative engages HBCU Computer Science Faculty with workshops aligning computer science curriculum with industry workforce needs and demands. Carita is a passionate advocate and champion for diversity in tech for underrepresented minorities and women. She is cofounder of an UNCF Affinity Group—Young Professional Development Group with support from key executive leaders. On September 2015, Carita co-organized the first annual Young, Black & Innovative event in partnership with General Assembly connecting 10 Black Startups to over 600 Black consumers during the 2015 Congressional Black Caucus Conference.

She is also a member of the White House Science and Technology 2015-16 "My Brothers Keeper's" STEM Taskforce and Maker Alliance as well as the White House Conference on Inclusive STEM Education for Youth of Color and Girls.

For six years, Carita managed the UNCF/Merck Science Initiative, a 20-year partnership with The Merck Foundation and UNCF aimed at providing scholarship, fellowship and academic support to African Americans Scientists where over 300 recipients now hold PhDs. In total, Carita has submitted over 11 million dollars in scholarship funding to 503 students.

Carita is a self-starter and macro thinker focused on streamlining ideas serving as an Intrapreneur, building new initiatives and disrupting the norm. Her core passion focuses on diversity and inclusion and exposing underrepresented minorities to key opportunities that advances their career. Her career has been marked by STEM engagement and professional development programs that innovate empower and connect minorities to key opportunities that advances their careers.

# Emancipation Proclamation (1863)

*"Do you know who is at the moment the largest slaveholder in the United States?"*

— CHARLES SUMNER

THE EMANCIPATION PROCLAMATION is inarguably one of the most important documents in American history. On January 1ˢᵗ, 1863, Abraham Lincoln drafted and signed the executive order, ending slavery in 10 Confederate states.[33]

Lincoln's primary goal was to take advantage of the rebellion in the South known as the Civil War. His purpose was to free the slaves and disarm the South. Southern economy was based on slavery. Slaves were used for transporting goods, agricultural labor, household labor and much more. Thus, Lincoln found ending slavery to be a direct way to cripple the South's production methods.

It was a strange decision that shocked his cabinet. Many called it a bold move that they struggled to understand. Given that it was wartime, he had the ability to use wartime powers to enforce special laws. The Emancipation Proclamation was one of those laws!

By 1862, DC reflected a tale of two cities. It was a "thriving center for slavery and the slave trade, and a hub of anti-slavery activity among abolitionists

---

33 Immediate Effects of the Emancipation Proclamation https://hsp.org/education/unit-plans/the-immediate-effects-of-the-emancipation-proclamation

of all colors. Members of Congress represented states in which slavery was the backbone of the economy, and those in which slavery was illegal."[34]

That year, Charles Sumner of Massachusetts asked President Lincoln "Do you know who is at the moment the largest slaveholder in the United States?" Sumner went on the inform Lincoln that he was the largest slaveholder, not just by his own personal stock of slaves, but because the President "holds all the slaves of the District of Columbia."[35]

The DC Compensated Emancipation Act was passed as a compromise from President Lincoln. This Act freed 3,100 slaves in Washington, DC and "reimbursed those who had legally owned them and offered the newly freed women and men money to emigrate." April 16th date is celebrated as DC Emancipation Day. The Compensated Emancipation Act was a landmark achievement and integral part to the larger struggle of freedom.

Less than one year after the DC Emancipation Act, on January 1, 1863, President Lincoln issued the final Emancipation Proclamation. As a result, former slaves were then invited to serve in combat in the Union Army - another smart move. Slaves were more than happy to legally pick up arms and attack their former slave masters. By the end of the war, the Northern Army held 200,000 Blacks fighting for them.

Prior to this maneuver, Lincoln held the position that each state should govern its own slavery laws. However, deep in his heart, he always felt that slavery was wrong. The Emancipation Proclamation served to accomplish many of his interests at the same time and established him as a staunch abolitionist.

The document excluded slave holding border states such as Maryland, Delaware, Missouri and Kentucky — "out of fear of sending them into rebellion. Enslaved people living in states controlled by the Confederacy could only be freed if and when the Union Army arrived and liberated them in

---

34 Ending Slavery in the District of Columbia https://emancipation.dc.gov/page/ending-slavery-district-columbia

35 Ending Slavery in the District of Columbia https://emancipation.dc.gov/page/ending-slavery-district-columbia

person."[36] Nevertheless, the Proclamation clearly stated that slavery would end in states that refused to join the Union.

The Emancipation Proclamation was read under an oak tree at what is now Hampton University.

The Confederates entered a state of disrepair upon hearing the news. As the North advanced further into the South they captured slaves as contraband. Upon their Emancipation, all slaves were freed at the stroke of midnight. Unlike in some other countries when slavery has ended, there was no offer of compensation to the slave-owners, leaving them to feel deprived of what they believed to be their property. Between losing its precious gems and the additional troops entering daily from the North, Southern plantation owners found themselves in a rough spot and many even fled their homes.

While the Emancipation Proclamation serves as the statement in history that marked the end, slavery did not officially end in the United States until 1865. Since Lincoln passed the original measure during wartime, it had not passed by Congress and left the status of freedom for the slaves unclear.

Most slaves were not free until after the war had concluded. Six months after the last surrendering of the Confederacy, Congress passed the 13th Amendment to the US Constitution, finally outlawing slavery throughout the entire country.

The Amendment stated that:

*"neither slavery nor involuntary servitude, except as a punishment for crime whereof the party shall have been duly convicted, shall exist within the United States, or any place subject to their jurisdiction."*

This Amendment lead to the freedom of 3.1 million slaves.[37] The first Emancipation Parade was hosted in Washington, DC on April 19, 1886, four years at the DC Emancipation Act.

---

36 Ending Slavery in the District of Columbia https://emancipation.dc.gov/page/ending-slavery-district-columbia

37 Effects of the Emancipation Proclamation http://historycooperative.org/effects-emancipation-proclamation/

# Harriet Tubman (1820 – 1913)
Soldier, Nurse, Spy, Emancipation Activist

Araminta Harriet Tubman was born in Dorchester County, Maryland to enslaved parents, Harriet "Rit" Green and Ben Boss. Harriet was one of nine children born between 1820 and 1825.

During her early child hood her master's son sold three of her sisters and she suffered severe violence. Constant lashings left permanent scars and an incessant headache.

As a teen, she was once sent to the store where she came across an escaped slave. The man's master told Harriet to catch him but she refused to which he threw a two-pound weight at her head. This left her with seizures, headaches and narcoleptic episodes for the rest of her life.

When Harriet's father was 45 he was set free upon his owner's death. However, he still decided to work for his former owners' family. Sadly, Rit and her children were also to be set free under similar circumstances but the family choose not to free them.

By the time Harriet was an adult, half of the Blacks in Eastern Shore, Maryland were free. Oftentimes families would be comprised of freedmen and slaves. Harriet herself married a freedman named John Tubman in 1844. Since Harriet was still a slave, any children she had would also be considered slaves since the mother set the precedent of the offspring.

Shortly after marriage and a few disputes over traveling North, Harriet escaped from slavery with her two brothers in 1849. Around that time her owner passed and she seized the opportunity to run. As a slave that was low on the totem pole of her plantation, she feared that the family may sell her once the dust settled. A public offering for $300 was posted for the return of Araminta, Harry and Ben. Missing their family and having second thoughts, the brothers wanted to return to the plantation. Harriet brought her brothers back to the plantation but decided she could no longer remain a slave at left for Pennsylvania alone.

Leveraging the Underground Railroad to travel 90 miles to Philadelphia she felt a sense of relief when crossing into Pennsylvania. Harriet once said "when I found I had crossed that line, I looked at my hands to see if I was the same person. There was such a glory over everything; the sun came like gold through the trees, and over the fields, and I felt like I was in Heaven."

Feeling unsettled that she was free while her family members were still slaves, she decided she wouldn't rest until she freed her family. The opportunity arose in 1850 when Harriet was warned that her niece was about to be sold along with her two children. She then assisted John Bowley, a free black man and her niece, Kessiah's, husband to make the winning bid for his wife at an auction in Baltimore and then guided them back to Philly. This was the first of many trips Harriet would make to free her family and others. Interestingly, of the hundreds of slaves she freed, her husband declined to go and stayed in Maryland, with his new wife.

Around this same time, the Fugitive Slave Law passed that allowed captured slaves in the North to be returned to slavery. This led to a rise in former slaves and free Blacks being sold to the South. Northern police were forced to help capture former slaves, regardless of their personal objections. Staying one step ahead, Harriet changed the ending destination of the Underground Railroad to Canada, which prohibited slavery.

Things really kicked off in 1851 when Harriet helped free 11 slaves, stopping at Frederick Douglass' house along the way. Douglass writes in his book that it was during this visit that he depleted his savings to help Harriet and the slaves unbeknownst to them.

Abolitionist John Brown entered Harriet's life in 1858. He was a staunch advocate against slavery and died in the name of disrupting the institution. Sharing his goal, but feeling his method could sometimes be extreme, Harriet firmly supported John. Harriet says she received a vision about John before they ever met. He made Harriet into a General and called on her to assist with an attack on slaveholders at Harper's Ferry. However, Harriet was suffering from a severe headache at the time and did not arrive in time to assist him. Ending in defeat, John Brown was executed as a martyr.

Highly active in the military during the Civil War, Harriet started as a cook and nurse but quickly rose to armed scout and spy. *Harriet Tubman was the first woman to lead an armed expedition in the war*, guiding the Combahee River Raid in South Carolina to free 700 slaves.

Barely 10 years after her freedom, in 1859, Senator Seward sold Harriet a small piece of land in Auburn, New York. It became a safe-haven for her family and friends. After the war, she resided there and married a Civil War veteran named Nelson Davis, adopting a baby girl named Gertie.

Due to her disputes over pay equality during her service in the military, Harriet collected little to no wages leaving her financially vulnerable. Her mother would complain that all the accolades Harriet received did not feed their family. With her health ailing, one of her neighbors, Sarah Bradford, decided to write a book about Harriet's life, *Scenes in the Life of Harriet Tubman*. Sarah dedicated the money from the book to Harriet's family.

Nevertheless, Harriet continued to give and help as many people as possible. In 1903, she donated a piece of her property to the African Methodist Episcopal church in Auburn. In 1908, the Harriet Tubman Home for the Aged also opened on this land where she died of pneumonia in 1913.

Harriet was buried with military honors at Fort Hill Cemetery in Auburn. She is named the 3rd most influential American before the Civil War. Dozens of schools have been erected in her honor and she now graces the United States $20 bill.

The US Treasury Department announced in April 2016 that Harriet Tubman will replace Andrew Jackson on $20 bill to #BreakThePaperCeiling. "Secretary Lew's choice of the freed slave and freedom fighter Harriet Tubman to one day feature on the $20 note is an exciting one, especially given that she emerged as the choice of more than half a million voters in our online poll last Spring. Not only did she devote her life to racial equality, she fought for women's rights alongside the nation's leading suffragists" as stated by the Women on 20s' campaign.[38]

America's decision to feature Harriet on the $20 bill, replacing the slaveholder Jackson who served at the helm of removing Native Americans from their homes, is a step in the right direction.

---

38  Harriet Tubman Biography http://www.biography.com/people/harriet-tubman-9511430

# Erin Horne McKinney

Co-Founder, Black Female Founders

*Branding and progressing Black founders*

Passionate about emerging technology, entrepreneurship, and social justice, Erin Horne McKinney is the co-founder of Black Female Founders (#BFF) and KissIntel app. She previously served as Senior Advisor on Innovation and Entrepreneurship to D.C.'s Deputy Mayor for Greater Economic Opportunity (DMGEO). Erin is a serial entrepreneur and intrapreneur with nearly two decades of tech policy, marketing communications, economic and business development experience.

Prior to joining DMGEO, Erin served as D.C.'s Tech and Innovation Sector Manager within the Office of the Deputy Mayor for Planning and Economic Development (DMPED) representing technology firms, entrepreneurs, and organizations. In this role, she created innovative branding practices to build what is now the DC startup ecosystem. Her worked served as a template for DC and other urban cities to build a quality, sustainable tech network with community leaders.

Erin has held leadership roles with the National Association of Multicultural Digital Entrepreneurs (NAMDE) and the Maynard Institute. Her telecommunications policy work includes research positions with TechNet, the National Telecommunication and Information Administration within the U.S. Department of Commerce, and the National Black Caucus of State Legislators. As a marketing and communications consultant specializing in business development and diversity marketing, Erin produced programs for organizations such as General Mills, the City of Minneapolis, and IPX International. She also generated and managed millions of dollars for companies such as ABC Radio, CBS Radio, and Clear Channel Communications as a top national media strategist. Additionally, Erin worked in the communications and editorial departments of Marriott International, TIME magazine, BET News, and Knight-Ridder Newspapers.

Erin is a mentor at 1776, WeWork, and AccelerateDC. She also serves on the Byte Back board, the Halcyon Incubator advisory board, and the Fish & Richardson's FISHstep program review committee. Erin is a doctoral student in the communications technology policy program at Howard University, where she also completed her BA and MA.

# Sharecropper Economics (1865)

*I am in earnest - I will not equivocate - I will not*
*excuse - I will not retreat a single inch*
*- and I will be heard*

— WILLIAM LLOYD GARRISON

As BLACK CODES and Jim Crow laws grew in the south, most newly emancipated Blacks depended on sharecropping to gain financial stability.

Many people falsely assume that slavery ended with the Civil War and Emancipation Proclamation. People mistakenly feel the scars of slavery are not fresh and should only be discussed in classrooms. Yet, it couldn't be further from the truth because in a sense, slavery has never really ended. It simply took on new forms – including sharecropping and the convict lease system, which kept Blacks as slaves within the construct of leasing them to corporations.

A very short-lived Reconstruction era emerged after the Civil War ended. The era enjoyed Union troops filling former rebel states to ensure Blacks received equal rights, and a significant rise in Black politicians on both the local, state and federal levels. While Blacks were experiencing the time of their lives, a deep undercurrent of political tension was brewing from the economic recovery of the Black population.

# History of the Black Dollar

Due to the war, the entire South was suffering from economic woes due to the abolishment of slavery, making plantation owners must pay wages to their workers. However, the wage system was ripe with fraud and highly resembled the plantation system. Naturally, the former slaves were not ecstatic to work for subpar wages.

With the South in shambles and currency in limited supply, the confederate currency and wage-labor economy was pointless. The banking system was destroyed. Farmers and landowners could not borrow money. Most were left in economic ruins and very few could even gather collateral for loans. This period also produced poor harvest, further extenuating the problem as farmers were unable to secure enough crops to hire laborers. But none of this really mattered to Blacks because "freed people had altogether higher aspirations than being simply wage laborers on large, centrally-organized plantations."[39]

Congress established the Freedman's Bureau to aid former slaves, help refugees and manage abandoned land, and supervise labor contracts. Congress envisioned the Bureau "would undertake the role of umpire in ensuring that the contracts reflected the free interplay of market forces."[40] Commissioner Major General Oliver Howard was provided direct instructions on what contracts and terms could not be dictated by the Bureau.

The South's labor problem remained a mess as most farmers still felt Black laborers required supervision. Whitelaw Reid said that most people in the South believed that "niggers wouldn't do more 'n half as much, now that the lash was no longer behind them." So to ensure that Blacks would actually work "they sought to restore gang labor, centralized plantations, and the close supervision of the work and social lives of their new laborers, which to their mind, were central to the economics of plantation slavery."

While this system is obviously wrought with wrongs, it provided a small escape to autonomy for Blacks – providing them leverage to make sharecropping easier.

---

39 John J. McDermott, "Reconstruction and Post-Civil War Reconciliation," *Military Review* 89:1 (2009)

40 Ralph Shlomowitz, "The Origins of Southern Sharecropping," *Agricultural History* 53:3 (1979), pg 588

It is no mystery that during the harsh times of slavery, anyone from any Black family could be taken and sold without question, leaving no building blocks for the Black family. Insert freedom.

With the fresh ability to travel where their hearts' desired, Blacks started going through great lengths to connect with and reestablish their families. This deep-seated focused attempt to restore their families, redirecting labor to serve household needs, were the integral seeds of self-sufficiency that were needed to grow the world of sharecropping.

For an amazing period, there was a huge labor shortage in the South which gave former slaves the power to decisively contribute and work at will. This helped to contour the new labor system forcing centralized plantations to be split up into smaller plots of land, and chain gangs were replaced with family groups that managed the land.

This approach was enjoyed by the landowner and sharecropper. The land-owners managed to convince themselves that they created a group incentive scheme, and Blacks leveraged it as an opportunity for less oversight. Blacks also preferred this method because it "increased effectiveness of the incentives implicit in the share arrangement, more closely matching effort and reward at the individual family level, and in the preference that freedom showed for family farming over collective arrangements."

For the most part, sharecropping exploited Black farmers. Lacking resources to purchase supplies, sharecroppers would have to leverage their future crops as collateral for loans, almost always becoming bound to their merchants for long-term periods. This relationship also hindered sharecroppers from allowing other merchants to bid on their crops for the best price. This becomes further exasperated when sharecroppers must focus on cash crops to grow like cotton, instead of food, leaving them to need additional credit to feed their families. The situation becomes sadly laughable when you add in that merchants would charge ridiculous interest on credit for food and was the sole controller of the local food source. It doesn't take much to see how a sharecropper would quickly find himself in a perpetual cycle of debt that is in fact insurmountable to pay off. Hence, sharecroppers remained in "perpetual debt and slavery perpetuated itself; but rather than a physical slavery, it was an economic bondage that held Black people to the land."

Sharecroppers were gravely punished if their crops did not properly reap. It was commonly stated in sharecropper contracts that they must "pay for fifty acres of corn land at seven dollars per acre and ten acres of tobacco land at twelve dollars and fifty cents per acre in money" and others just dismissed them completely. With control of the contracts, landowners dominated sharecroppers' lives. "In some cases, if sickness or accident prevented sharecroppers from meeting their obligations, the landowner had the power to outsource the work at the sharecroppers' expense." White southerners maintained these terms "to hold freedmen, the large majority of whom became sharecroppers, in a subordinate status after emancipation. Yet, while Black sharecroppers in many ways remained subordinate to white landowners, the situation was worse for black women. For them, sharecropping combined the oppression of debt peonage and black patriarchy within the family."[41]

The difference in economic status between Blacks and whites is one of the most important social issues in modern US history. The relationships between race, education, employment and housing have become critical pillars of these bonds. Understanding these interrelationships in the context of history, helps to bring forth a higher level of empathy for the dynamics at play with the social and economic environments in which the context takes place.

In 1896, the US Supreme Court ruled that courts did not have the authority to "eradicate racial instincts or to abolish distinctions based upon physical difference."

# William Lloyd Garrison (1805 – 1879)
Abolitionist, Journalist, Suffragist, Social Reformer

William Lloyd Garrison, the son of a seaman, was born in Newburyport Massachusetts, in December, 1805. Apprenticed as a printer, he became editor of the Newburyport Herald in 1824. Four years later he was appointed editor of the National Philanthropist in Boston.

---

41   http://www.hamptoninstitution.org/sharecropping.html#_edn10

In 1828 Garrison met Benjamin Lundy, the Quaker anti-slavery editor of the Genius of Universal Emancipation. The following year he became co-editor of Lundy's newspaper. One article, where Garrison's criticism of a merchant involved in the slave-trade, resulted in him being imprisoned for libel.

Released in June 1830, Garrison's period in prison made him even more determined to bring an end to slavery. Whereas he previously shared Lundy's belief in gradual emancipation, Garrison now advocated "immediate and complete emancipation of all slaves." After breaking with Lundy, Garrison returned to Boston where he established his own anti-slavery newspaper, *The Liberator*. The newspaper's motto was: "Our country is the world - our countrymen are mankind"

In *The Liberator* Garrison not only attacked slave-holders but the "timidity, injustice and absurdity" of the gradualists. Garrison famously wrote: "I am in earnest - I will not equivocate - I will not excuse - I will not retreat a single inch - and I will be heard." The newspaper only had a circulation of 3,000 but the strong opinions expressed in its columns gained Garrison a national reputation as the leader of those favoring immediate emancipation.

Garrison's views were particularly unpopular in the South and the state of Georgia offered $5,000 for his arrest and conviction. Garrison was highly critical of the Church for its refusal to condemn slavery. Some anti-slavery campaigners began arguing that Garrison's bitter attacks on the clergy was frightening off potential supporters.

In 1832, Garrison formed the New England Anti-Slavery Society. The following year he helped organize the Anti-Slavery Society. Garrison was influenced by the ideas of Susan Anthony, Elizabeth Cady Stanton, Lucretia Mott, Lucy Stone and other feminists who joined the society. This was reflected in the content of the *Liberator* that now began to advocate women's suffrage, pacifism and temperance.[42]

*Extracted from Spartacus Education*

---

42  http://spartacus-educational.com/USASgarrison.htm

# Thomas Nida

Regional Executive, John Marshall Bank Board Chair, Charter Schools Development Corporation

Born in Southeast, DC, Thomas Nida has grown to be one of the most nationally trusted advisors to the financial, education and civil rights communities. With a 50-year career in banking and finance, Tom Nida currently serves as D.C. Regional Executive of John Marshall Bank, a local community bank. Tom's career has been focused on community development and non-profit financing, to include lending to D.C. public charter schools.

Nida has been very active in the charter school movement in Washington, DC, serving as a board member and treasurer of the Arts and Technology Academy Public Charter School, for which he helped obtain DC Revenue Bond, tax-exempt financing.

He was appointed to the DC Public Charter School Board by Mayor Anthony Williams in 2003, and was elected Chairman of the Board in 2004; serving in that capacity until February 2010.

Tom has served as a Board Member (and current Board Advisor) to the DC Association of Chartered Public Schools; as current Board Chair of the Charter Schools Development Corporation; and as a Board Member for the DC Students Construction Trades Foundation, which supports the Academy of Construction & Design at IDEA Public Charter High School.

He also has real estate development experience, having founded and managed several land trusts focused on renovation of historic commercial properties over the past twenty-four years, especially in urban communities. He leverages his position within the community to be a staunch advocate for preserving urban culture while increasing resources.

Tom is recognized nationally for his expertise in charter school financing, having authored a series of articles on charter school lending in The RMA Journal, a national financial publication.

Tom graduated from the University of Wisconsin and completed an Executive Program at the Darden Graduate School of Business at the University of Virginia

# Freedmen's Bank (1874)

*"The Legacy of The Freedman's Bank serves as a reminder that we must
continue striving for greater financial inclusion for all Americans"*

— SECRETARY JACOB LEW

THE FREEDMEN'S BANK was created by US Congress and the Freedmen's Bureau
on March 3, 1865 to help freedmen transition from slavery to freedom.

Before the emancipation, many Blacks in the border-states found freedom
in the Union Army and held employment. Northern abolitionists called for a
freedmen's bank to help ex-slaves develop financial responsibility.

During the Civil War, numerous small banks were established to receive
deposits from Black soldiers and runaway slaves working for the Union throughout the South. Deposit receipts would often get lost and it frequently prevented freedmen from retrieving their deposits. Also, when Blacks were killed in
battle and did not list a family relative, their deposits often went unclaimed.
Sometimes even when relatives were named, finding their location would be
even more difficult since the war disrupted so many families.

Congregational Minister John W. Alvord and A. M. Sperry, an abolitionist,
launched the Freedmen's Savings and Trust Company in 1864 to reduce banking inaccuracies and bring all deposits from Blacks under one large institution.
Congress passed legislation to incorporate the bank with President Lincoln
immediately signing the bill into law. "To support the land grants and other

elements of the Freedman's Bureau Act, a Freedman's Bank was established to help newly freed Americans navigate their financial lives.[43]" It was considered *the* financial literacy program for Blacks.

The bank only received deposits "by or on behalf of persons heretofore held in slavery in the United States, or their descendants."[44] Interestingly, up to 7% interest was allowed for deposits and unclaimed accounts were pooled into a charitable fund that was used to educate children of ex-slaves.

In 1868, Black staffers were trained to take over the bank's operations and headquarters was moved to Washington, DC. The new location was positioned across from the US Department of Treasury, in a grand building that cost $260,000 to construct. It's a little-known fact that Lincoln personally asked for it to be moved so that it could be close to him. His fondness for the bank would ultimately contribute to his demise.

Freedmen's bank was one of the first multi-state banks in the nation, with 37 branches in 17 states and DC at its highest moment of operation. By 1870 nearly all local branches were managed by Blacks. "At its height, the Bank had over $57 million in deposits (adjusted for inflation) and 70,000 depositors."[45]

Five weeks after the creation of the Freedmen's Bank, President Lincoln was assassinated.

Seven years later, in 1872, US Congress voted to permanently close the Freedman's Bureau. While the bank remained operational, economic instability ripened. People started to notice the large amount of fraud from upper management that was taking place at the bank, bringing it down and creating The Panic of 1873. To save the bank, Frederick Douglass was elected president in 1874.

When Douglass arrived at the Bank in Washington, DC he wrote:

*"The whole thing was beautiful. I had read of this bank when I lived in Rochester, and had indeed been solicited to become one of its trustees, and had reluctantly consented to do so: but when I came to Washington and saw its magnificent brown stone front, its towering height, its perfect appointments, and the fine display it*

---

43  http://freedmansbank.org/

44  Claude F. Oubre, Forty Acres and a Mule: The Freedmen's Bureau and Black Land Ownership (Baton Rouge: The Louisiana State University Press, 1978), pp. 43, 68, 159-60

45  http://freedmansbank.org/

*made in the transaction of its business, I felt like the Queen of Sheba when she saw the riches of Solomon, that 'half had not been told me'."*

As President, Douglass found profound corruption within the bank and poorly calculated investments across industries being made with depositor savings. Desperate to cease the bank's instability and volatility, Douglas invested $10,000 of his personal savings. Sadly, this was for naught, as the bank could not compete with the political forces that destroyed the Reconstruction era. Although Douglas pleaded for Congress to intervene, on June 29, 1874, the bank was officially closed. At the date of closing $2,993,790.68 was due to 61,144 depositors, $48.72 on average[46]. In 2017, this would be equivalent to roughly $100m total, $1,500 on average due.

The federal government kept all the money, collapsing the bank and leaving all the account holders penniless. In Washington, DC alone over 3,000 depositors – both individuals and cultural institutions – lost their savings.

The tragedy of Freedmen's Bank left most Blacks with a huge feeling of distrust of the American banking system that is still prevalent in 2017. Nevertheless, the records of the bank depositors serve as a beautiful source for Black family researchers to better discover the progression of Blacks during the Reconstruction era that followed the American Civil War. In fact, 29 branches of Freedmen's Bank records are still available today and searchable via National Archives.

Interestingly, these records "are thousands of signature cards that contain personal data about the individual depositors. In addition to the names and ages of depositors, the files can contain their places of birth, residence, and occupations; names of parents, spouses, children, brothers, and sisters; and in some cases, the names of former slave owners. These records of the individuals, who lived through the transition from slavery to freedom, are the keys that allow their descendants to unlock the mysteries of their largely undocumented family histories.

Within these records are stories that reveal struggle, sacrifice, courage and determination; stories that must be told to our children and left for future generations."[47]

---

46  Walter L. Fleming, The Freedmen's Saving Bank: A Chapter in the Economic History of the Negro Race (Chapel Hill: The University of North Carolina Press, 1927)

47  http://freedmansbank.org/

In 1879, Blanche Kelso Bruce became the first Black and only former slave to preside over the US Senate. He was also the first Black whose signature appeared on currency as Register of the Treasury in 1881. In 1888, Capital Savings Bank became the first bank founded and operated by Blacks.

On January 7, 2016, with the assistance of former Mayor of Atlanta and Sr. Advisor to Martin Luther King Jr., Secretary Lew publicly renamed the Treasury Annex Building, The Freedman's Bank Building, in honor of the site where the Freedman's Saving Bank once stood.

# Frederick Douglass (1818 – 1895)
Author, Government Official, and Civil Rights Activist

Frederick Augustus Washington Bailey was born a slave in Talbot County Maryland. Like most slaves, the date of birth is unknown. Later in life he chose February 14th as his day of celebration. Raised by his grandmother, Betty Bailey, he was invited to be a house slave at a young age. His mother died when he was 10 and he seldom saw her.

As a pre-teen, Frederick was sent to Baltimore to live with his master's brother Hugh Auld. His wife, Sophia, taught Frederick to read and write when he was 12. When Hugh found out he was very upset at the chance of his neighbors discovering his family was breaking the law so he forbad his wife from continuing the lessons. That said, Frederick began to teach himself through conversations and small lessons with white children.

His education grew stronger by the day and his hate of slavery by the night. He would read any newspaper he could get his hands on to stay abreast of the latest happenings of the abolition movement. *The Columbian Orator* was his favorite newspaper and he credits it for helping to shape his views on human rights. Once he grew to articulate his knowledge, he would share everything he learned daily with other slaves.

When William Freeland hired him to work his plantation, he taught the surrounding slaves on the planation how to read the New Testament during church. However, his talent and their thirst of learning drew such large crowds that other slave owners became upset, despite Freeland himself not really caring. Strategizing against Fredericks' church lessons, the local KKK attacked the slaves one Sunday morning, indefinitely disbanding the church.

He was forced to work for Edward Covey who was known as the 'slave breaker.' He consistently abused Frederick in the worst way, daily, at the mere age of 16. While his body eventually gave in to the demands, he never controlled Frederick's mind. Reaching his breaking point, Frederick fought back in a vigorous scene. Covey lost to the strong Frederick, choosing not to mention it to anyone out of fear of losing his reputation and thus means of living. Covey never beat him again.

After getting into an altercation with his actual master shortly thereafter and facing the threat of being sold, Hugh Auld purchased Frederick in exchange for clearing his brother's debt to him. While appreciative, Frederick had only one subject on his mind: freedom.

On September 3, 1868, Frederick Douglass, a slave, boarded the train in Havre de Grace, Maryland. He attempted escaping twice before he was successful. His girlfriend, Anna Murray, a free black woman in Baltimore, helped him with his final attempt. She gave him some money and a sailor's uniform. He had a friend that traveled often as a free Black seaman and borrowed his identification papers. Once safe on the train and in slight disbelief of the ease of his execution, he made it to abolitionist David Ruggles' house in New York in less than 24 hours.

Upon arrival, Frederick sent for Anna to meet him in New York and married her on September 15, 1838 as two free people! They married under the name Johnson to hide Douglass's identity, settling in New Bedford, Massachusetts, an up and coming Black community. Once at peace, they returned to the name Douglass and joined a Black church that held regular abolitionist meetings. *The Liberator*, William Lloyd Garrison's weekly journal, became his favorite publication.

His community began to recognize him as an anti-slavery lecturer and asked him to share his history at abolitionist meetings as representative for slaves since he was very articulate and well read. Garrison himself was impressed with Frederick and wrote about him in *The Liberator*. A few days after the release, Frederick gave his first public speech at the Massachusetts Anti-Slavery

Society's annual convention in Nantucket. Initially and throughout his career, crowds would often greet him in very hostile manners. For instance, in 1843, he was chased and beaten by an angry mob prior to being rescued by a local Quaker family.

With Garrison's support, Frederick published his first autobiography in 1845, *Narrative of the Life of Frederick Douglass, an American Slave.* It was a best seller and translated into several European languages. Critics found it hard to believe that a slave with no formal education could have produced such a masterpiece.

Additionally, he published other autobiographies such as *My Bondage and My Freedom* in 1855 and *Life and Times of Frederick Douglas* in 1881. With such high press of his autobiography reaching the masters he escaped from, he was forced to escape overseas to avoid being recaptured. On August 16, 1845, he set sail for Liverpool and arrived in Ireland at the onset of the Potato Famine. He stayed in Ireland and Britain for two years with his wife and immediately grew fame abroad speaking to large audiences about slavery. Magnetized by his stories, supporters gave him money to purchase his legal freedom and in 1847 he returned to the United States as a free man.

With a new found and real sense of freedom, Frederick began publishing abolitionist newspapers to include *The North Star, Frederick Douglass Weekly, Frederick Douglass' Paper, Douglass' Monthly* and *New National Era*. The North Star, his famed paper that continued in print well after his death, held the motto "Right is of no Sex – Truth is of no Color – God is the Father of us all, and we are all brethren."

As a big supporter of women's rights, he became the only African American to attend the first women's rights convention at Seneca Falls, New York. Elizabeth Cady Stanton, his friend, asked the assembly to "pass a resolution stating the goal of the women's suffrage."[48] While many opposed Elizabeth, Douglass stood up for her, eloquently outlining the issues and arguing that he could not accept being able to vote as a Black man if women could not also have that right. The resolution passed.

By the arrival of the Civil War, Frederick was one of the most famous Black people in the country. In 1863, President Lincoln spoke with Frederick about

---

48 Frederick Douglass Biography http://www.biography.com/people/frederick-douglass-9278324

the treatment of Black soldiers and later President Johnson referred to him on Black suffrage.

With the major support of Frederick Douglass, the Emancipation Proclamation freed all slaves. Although this was led by Lincoln, Frederick supported John C. Fremont in the 1864 election because he was disappointed that Lincoln did not publicly endorse suffrage for Black freedmen.

After the war, Frederick served as president of the Freedman's Savings Bank and purchased a mansion in DC that serves as a museum today. After resigning from that position, he was appointed minister-resident and consul-general to the Republic of Haiti. He also became the first Black to be nominated for Vice President of the United States. He was Victoria Woodhull's running mate on the Equal Rights Party ticket in 1872. It was the first time a Black had appeared on the presidential ballot.

Frederick and his wife Anna had five children: Rosetta, Lewis, Henry, Frederick Jr., Charles and Annie. Interestingly, Frederick was a bit of a player and began to have marital strife. After Anna's death, he married a white feminist from Honeoye, New York. They remained together for 11 years until his death.

On February 20, 1895, after attending a meeting for the National Council of Negro Women in Washington, DC, Frederick Douglass died of a massive heart attack or stroke. He is buried in Mount Hope Cemetery in Rochester, New York.

# Rodney Williams
Founder, Lisnr

*Rodney Williams, CEO and Founder of LISNR, leads one of the most disruptive companies in mobile connectivity and the Internet of Things. In this column, Rodney will share his experiences leaving a Fortune 500 company to build his company from the ground up in the Midwest, provide his perspective on startup leadership and give tips and tricks to help other entrepreneurs starting their journey.*

In order to get to my big idea, which eventually became LISNR, I had a lot of practice generating big ideas for other people. At P&G, I was a brand manager for Pampers, meaning I oversaw all aspects of the brand and product and used technology to solve problems. Sometimes, I had to create my own solutions that I patented. By the time I was 27, I had 3 patents under my belt and won 9 awards, including the AdAge 40 Under 40 for my work with P&G.

Once I knew how to replicate my success with technology and patents, I continued to look for opportunities. Most marketers know by now that consumers are actively avoiding ads that are not shown at the right place or time. I wanted to figure out how to make advertising more effective. More than anything, an advertising effort is best received by consumers in a contextually relevant time and place. Figuring out how to achieve that perfect mix is the holy grail of marketing.

My aha moment came one day at lunch, during a routine, intense brainstorm. I wrote down three pages defining my idea, each one building on the other. "Sound can do more" became "morse code you can't hear" became "Sound you can't hear, connecting to consumers where they are". Reading those pages now makes me laugh – knowing what I do now, most of the ideas I wrote are still defining features of LISNR.

Eventually, I arrived around how to conceptually bring the idea to life as a business. Use inaudible sound waves to send content to fans' phones through music & live events. Conceptually, people enjoy when they get a exclusive content or personal message from their favorite artist based on their listen wherever they are. I felt I could bring a strong value proposition to the music industry and investors would resonate with my approach within this market.

The same day, I emailed Chris Ostoich, the only "startup" person I knew, and pitched him my idea. We went back and forth, fleshing out the idea as I explained it. Once Chris understood the concept, he thought this was a huge idea as well. We always knew this idea was bigger than music but in the early day music made people understand what we were up to.

Once I had my first co-founder, we realized we needed to find someone technical to help get this idea built. One of Chris's neighbors was an engineer, and so we immediately went over to his apartment and asked for guidance. He mentioned it would be costly to build, but if we were to bring it on the StartupBus, a startup competition on a bus on the way to SXSW, that he would help see where it goes. I applied and was accepted to be on the StartupBus. I also asked for a week and a half off work on super short notice (my boss at the time wasn't too happy about it, but he saw my passion).

*Extracted from Rodney Williams, Forbes*

# The Great
# Migration (1900)

*Millions of Blacks left the South for safety, higher
equality and better paying jobs in the North*

THERE WAS A major geographical shift in the Black population during the period
known as The Great Migration from 1910 to 1970, where millions of Blacks
left the South for safety, higher equality and better paying jobs in the North.
Blacks were growing irritated by the injustices of the South and wanted greater
opportunities.

In the early 1900s, America became characterized by the Jim Crow laws
that was starting to have an iron clad grip on the South. Segregation laws
helped whites maintain their dominance over Blacks. Schools, hospitals, voting stations, transportation, subway stations, bathrooms, restaurants, neighborhoods, phone booths, water fountains and even how high you could hold your
head while walking were all dictated by these laws. They formed an elaborate,
purposeful and impactful expression of white sovereignty that fed directly into
the image of the despicable Negro. While segregation legally began in 1889, the
Jim Crow laws of the early 20th century, embellished the physical and mental
separation.

Between 1880 and 1940, the Tuskegee Institute recorded 3,445 known
lynchings of Blacks. According to the National Association for the Advancement
of Colored People (NAACP), lynching is defined as: evidence exists that someone was killed, the person was killed in an illegal fashion, a group of three or

more people participated in the killing and the group acted out of a perception of service to justice or tradition.

To survive, Blacks collectively turned to self-defense, which often ended with physical conflict. 88% of lynchings took place in the South and usually involved an alleged rape by a Black person.

Despite living in a country that demanded equality to all, Blacks were forced into an unequal status. Blacks were referred to as socio-politically and biologically inferior. For example, in the 1920 Yale Review, Vernon Kellogg states "we prefer the characteristics of the white race, taken as a whole, to those of any other primary race… some of the results of such biological consideration of racial crossing are already known… the white and Black cross seems usually superior to the original Black parent type, although inferior to the white parent type."

In another example of 1906, President Theodore Roosevelt states in his memoirs that "the race cannot expect to get everything at once. It must learn to wait and bide its time, to prove itself worthy by showing its possession of perseverance, of thrift, of self-control."

The Great Migration caused unprecedented conflict in the workplace as Blacks offered higher quality performance for lower wages than whites. Inadequate housing facilities that were becoming increasingly overcrowded also frustrated Blacks and made them less tolerant of inferior treatment. Economic deprivation and a lack of political participation mixed with newly experienced Black soldiers that lost limbs for freedom, created a beautifully, dangerous combination for Black progress.

During the war, many whites were sent overseas, which opened thousands of jobs for Blacks that previously could not obtain them. As they returned home, they found their jobs had been taken and grew resentful against Blacks, leading to a series of riots on Black wealth from 1917 to 1960 in cities such as Houston, St. Louis, Chicago, DC, Detroit, Harlem, Los Angeles, Cleveland, Tulsa and Newark. The common denominators in all these cities had been the Black population shift, career advancement for Blacks, surge of violence, and military release.

In California, the Black population grew in urban cities. Racial discrimination forced men into service jobs such as shoe shining and chauffeuring. In

1907, Oakland hosted its 13th annual meeting of the Afro-American Council, showcasing the presence of a thriving middle class.[49]

Working hard and blessed with good fortune, many Black entrepreneurs, including women, began to climb the ladder of success. "Former slave Biddy Mason used the money she earned as a nurse to invest in Los Angeles real estate, becoming a wealthy philanthropist and founding the First AME Church. Mary Ellen Pleasant, another former slave, ran several businesses and restaurants in San Francisco, using her resources to fight for civil rights."

Many Blacks moved to Los Angeles, finding housing in Little Tokyo's Bronzeville, a former Japanese American neighborhood. Most homes and apartments were left vacant from residents being incarcerated in internment camps. "Racist real estate policies, including restrictive covenants, limited their ability to move out of segregated urban neighborhoods. Discrimination restricted their access to skilled and professional jobs as well as to higher education." Having just returned home from fighting a war, Black veterans saw the fight for freedom at home ever more important.

# Booker T. Washington (1856 – 1915)
Educator, University President, Community Builder

Booker Taliaferro Washington was born a slave in Franklin County, Virginia. While he did not know his exact birth date, it is now widely understood that he was born on April 5, 1856. His mother's name was Jane and his father was a white man from a local plantation.

When Booker was young, his job was carrying 100 pound sacks of grain to the plantation's mill. At that time, he had witnessed some white kids inside of a school, learning. He yearned for the opportunity but realized he was a slave and wasn't allowed to read.

Before reaching adolescence, the slaves were set free by the Emancipation Proclamation. Shortly after being freed at the age of 9, he moved with his

---

49 The Struggle for Economic Equality https://calisphere.org/exhibitions/48/african-americans-economic-equality/

mother to West Virginia. There, she married a freedman named Washington Ferguson. Living in poverty, Booker's stepfather forced him to work at the salt furnace. His mother, understanding his love of learning, got him a book for him to learn how to read. With this book, he would open a new educated world for himself. He rose almost every morning at 4am to study.

He graduated to houseboy for Viola Ruffner, a coal mine owner's wife, in 1866. Although she held a prodigious reputation for being pugnacious, she saw something in Booker and allowed him to go to school for an hour a day during the winter.

When he started grammar school he noted his nick name as his first name, Booker, and added Washington after George Washington, to make himself sound prestigious according to his autobiography, *Up From Slavery.*

In 1872, Booker T. Washington walked 500 miles to reach Hampton Normal and Agriculture Institute, now Hampton University, at the age of 16 in Hampton, Virginia. He picked up odd jobs to support himself along his journey.

Most interestingly, upon reaching Richmond, he slept in a cross space on the ground for a week. He paused here so that he could hold employment at the local port and gain enough money to finish the trip to Hampton.

Upon arriving at the now #1 HBCU in the world, with nothing but a toothbrush – a mandatory requirement regardless of financial means as a sign of being civilized - he begged the illustrious school to admit him. He was handed a broom and asked to sweep the floor as a test of his ambition. Feeling like his future laid in the power of that broom, he meticulously swept the floor. He was admitted to the school and served as janitor to pay for tuition. The standards of cleanliness that Booker T. introduced are still maintained to this day at Hampton.

Taking a liking to his effort, Hampton's founder, General Samuel C. Armstrong offered him a scholarship. Armstrong was a former commander of the Union Black regiment during the Civil War and a strong advocate for educating freed slaves. He became Booker's mentor and later, friend.

Booker T. graduated from Hampton in 1875 and was selected to speak at Hampton's graduation in 1879. Following his speech, General Armstrong offered Booker T. the opportunity to teach at Hampton.

After being a great steward of the school, Armstrong recommended him to run the newly developed Tuskegee Normal and Industrial Institute, now known as Tuskegee University. This was a big move for Black America as Armstrong was requested to send a white man. Instead, he noted that he knew no better man and sent Booker T. on his way.

Classes were first held in an old church, without funding, while Booker T. traveled the country to raise money. He carefully assured whites that Tuskegee would not interfere with their economics.

Under Booker T.'s leadership, Tuskegee rose to become one of the best schools in the country. Before he died, he helped erect 100 buildings, support 1,500 students, hired a 200-member faculty teaching 38 trades and raised nearly $2 million for the school.[50]

He personally shaped the curriculum, facilities and overall attitude of the students. The students respected him so much that during the early years, upperclassmen would volunteer to give up their dorm to sleep outside to allow more room for freshmen. They sometimes would wake up frostbitten from the cold.

In 1895, he was famously invited to speak at the Cotton States Exposition in Atlanta, Georgia – the first time a Black man had publicly addressed whites on such a large platform. During this speech, he advocated that Blacks could gain their constitutional rights through their own economic merit by becoming proficient at skills such as farming, carpentry, and masonry rather than pursuing legal and political means for collective advancement.

Creating a lot of controversy for himself, Booker T. "taught that economic stress for African Americans would take time, and that subordination to whites was a necessary evil until African Americans could prove they were worthy of full economic and political rights."[51]

In 1901, he was invited to the White House by President Theodore Roosevelt, making him the first Black after the abolition of slavery to be invited. Roosevelt and Taft both grew to rely on him as advisors on racial matters, primarily because he was an advocate for 'racial subservice.' That same year,

---

50 Booker T. Washington http://www.biography.com/people/booker-t-washington-9524663
51 Booker T. Washington http://www.biography.com/people/booker-t-washington-9524663

he published *Up From Slavery*, his autobiography and one of the most widely read books on the slave movement.

Sadly, with prominent Blacks such as Du Bois calling him a traitor for taking a back seat to whites, Booker T. lost most of his influence by 1913. The new, Wilson administration, sided more with Du Bois and wanted to promote Black equality.

Booker T. Washington remained the head of Tuskegee until his death on November 14, 1915. He passed at the age of 59 due to heart failure.

# Dawn Dickson
Founder, Flat Out Heels

*Migrating in comfort and style*

Dawn Dickson is on a mission to save women's feet, and so far it's working.

As CEO and founder of Flat Out of Heels, Dickson has sold more than 50,000 pairs of foldable women's flats since launching her product line in 2012.

"I was out one night, and my feet were killing me," the former marketing consultant said. "I just thought to myself, I wish I could get flats out of a vending machine."

A couple months later, in 2011, she began her Miami-based business with $10,000 from a friend to get it off the ground. An initial test run of 2,000 pairs on her Facebook page presented an early challenge.

"I realized the shoes weren't really good for anything but emergencies. They weren't that comfortable. They weren't durable. They just weren't a good shoe," she said, adding that she donated the remaining pairs to charity.

After going back to the drawing board, the 37-year-old retooled the product with higher-quality fabric and soles and launched her signature collection. Prices range from $19.99 to $29.99.

While Dickson originally envisioned the company selling primarily through vending machines, they currently comprise just a fraction of sales.

# History of the Black Dollar

About 85 percent of sales come via e-commerce, including Amazon.com. The remainder comes from specialty boutique locations and three vending machines across the nation.

Dickson is planning to roll out additional vending machines, currently being manufactured through her other start-up, Solutions Vending International, an automated retail systems designer that creates custom vending machines.

Dickson launched SVI after a bad experience with a supplier. Her machines offer wireless cashless payment systems and an online interface that allows businesses to track sales and monitor inventory remotely. Once her custom Flat Out machines are available, she will install them in nightclubs, airports and convention centers, where women often find themselves in search of comfortable shoes.

Dickson's shift from selling solely through vending machines to e-commerce has been crucial to building a profitable company. Celebrities like Vanessa Williams and Nancy O'Dell have been spotted in her flats, and Dickson recently earned second place and a $20,000 prize in the Small Business Administration's InnovateHER contest.

"Never be attached to one thing so closely that you can't pivot and adapt," she said.

Even though Dickson had to adapt her business model, she stood by her original goal of creating comfortable foldable shoes.

"Stick to your mission, even if it takes a different path to get there," she said.

Dickson describes herself as a serial entrepreneur. Her two businesses, Flat Out and SVI, currently employ about 15 people.

Yet while the road to success hasn't always been easy, Dickson says even tight situations have always worked out.

"Never give up, no matter what. There's definitely lots of dark days — especially in the beginning," she said.

*Extracted from Katie Little, CNBC*

# Convict Leasing (1909)

*The point of retracing this history is not to argue that prisons*
*have been a direct outgrowth of slavery, but to interrogate the*
*persistent connections between racism and the global economy*

IN 1909, THE state of Texas opened the Imperial State Prison Farm, one of the very first penal institutions in Texas on land that previously belonged to Imperial Sugar. It was renamed the Central State Prison Farm in 1930.

"At the end of the Civil War, Cunningham's purchase of what used to be "Oakland Plantations" shaped much of what Sugar Land has become today. He invested more than $1 million into the property, developing a sugar mill and a sugar refinery, and a town began to form around it. At the time, much of the workforce was made up of convicts that were leased from prison farms. After slavery was outlawed by the 13th Amendment, Blacks in America were incarcerated at far higher rates than their white contemporaries. These men and women were commonly leased to work on plantations such as Cunningham's. After Cunningham's plantation changed hands and became the home of the Imperial Sugar Company, the leasing of convicts continued."[52]

By 1950, over 5,000 acres had been acquired to house more than 1,000 inmates residing in Cunningham's – Central State Prison. This prison did not close until 2011, with the remaining inmates being sent to the nearby Jester State Prison Farm.

Connecting the dots between racism and criminalization after emancipation has been important to explaining the rise of industrialism. "The point of

---

52  What is the History of Convict Leasing in Sugar Land? https://exhibits.library.rice.edu/exhibits/show/sugarlandconvictleasing/history-of-convict-leasing/history

retracing this history is not to argue that prisons have been a direct outgrowth of slavery, but to interrogate the persistent connections between racism and the global economy."[53] Mass imprisonment directly emulates slavery.

Since the emancipation, the US has placed large investments into trading humanity. The country has used mass imprisonment as an ineffective prescription for addiction, mental illness, economic discipline and social control. Wacquant, a scholar of the corrections industry, termed this as "the carceral management of poverty."

Caked into the 13th Amendment was the right to use prison labor as a bridge between slavery and paid work. When the 13th Amendment abolished slavery, it freed everyone "except as a punishment for crime." Thus, slavery has never ended in the prison system. This tiny stipulation provided the intellectual and legal means to allow the country to exasperate free labor by leasing prisoners to local businesses.

White Redeemers – planters, farmers and politicians – demanded racial order by through harsher Black Codes that increased penalties for petty crimes such as vagrancy, loitering and public drunkenness. While Blacks built schools, churches and social organizations such as the NAACP to fight for political participation, the Redeemers used state-sponsored violence to reduce the advancements made during the Reconstruction era.

"Mass imprisonment was employed as a means of coercing resistant freed slaves into becoming wage laborers. Prison populations soared during this period, enabling the state to play a critical role in mediating the brutal terms of negotiation between capitalism and the spectrum of unfree labor."[54]

The 13th Amendment moved American power from Washington, DC to individual states, changing the US political landscape. This move then allowed each state to regulate freedom by its own definition. At the same time, this move had the dual effect of helping Blacks to establish legal rights.

Convict labor grew increasingly racially based as it was a common assumption that Blacks were more suitable for hard physical labor for farms, railroads and construction company projects. This theme transferred into the actual

---

53 History is a Weapon http://www.historyisaweapon.com/defcon1/gilmoreprisonslavery.html

54 History is a Weapon http://www.historyisaweapon.com/defcon1/gilmoreprisonslavery.html

workforce and is still prevalent throughout companies today. For instance, in many waste management companies you will find Blacks as the primary laborers with whites primarily employed as drivers.

It is a little-known fact that not only Black men, but also Black women were forced to work on the front lines of hard labor, further revealing how closely this system mirrored slavery. This constant reminder of slavery comforted these Redeemers as they increasingly believed they could bring slavery back.

Despondently, these thoughts began to spread to the North who had historically focused on industrial labor. They seized an opportunity to expand their agriculture through the racially based prison system. These prisons were filled with victims that were criminalized for committing Black Code crimes.

While prime abolitionists made it impossible to retreat backwards to Slavery, racial labor movements continued in the form of convict labor. Once again on the backs of Blacks, this convict labor built the post-Civil War infrastructure throughout America.

Opposed to this "free unfree labor," labor unions, which hated prison labor, aggressively pushed against convict leasing. The Depression highlighted the very reason why labor unions took this so personally. Unionists felt that prison labor would further imperil a workforce that was already over capacity. And that is exactly what happened during the Depression.

To solve this problem, the corrections industry created a "state-use" system that only permitted prison labor for state projects. This eliminated the competition between convict and union labor, while still allowing states to use Blacks for free labor. This silenced the unions who mostly had their own self-interest at heart.

With local government in control, county sheriffs and judges became ridiculously powerful. Sheriffs immediately made deals with local farmers and contractors to lease out Black convicts, providing further incentives for them to lock up as many freedman as they could capture to keep a steady supply of labor.

Eventually full economies of scale formed around the prisons and convict leasing system (that still exist today), including a trade system for convict contracts.

"The witnesses and public officials who were owed portions of the lease payments earned by convicts received paper receipts – usually called scrips – from the county that could be redeemed only after the convict had generated enough money to pay them off. Rather than wait for the full amount, holders of scrips would sell their notes for cash to speculators at a lower than face amount. In return, the buyers were to receive the full lease payments – profiting handsomely from those convicts who survived, losing money on the short-lived."[55]

Taking it a step further, the Prison Industries Reorganization Administration, a New Deal project, hosted a study with all 50 states on prison labor to ultimately recommend the expansion of the prison system in every state. What is most fascinating is that there are no clear statistics that demonstrate that crime, especially violent crime, increased during this period. So, what was the basis for their growth forecasting?

Well, sadly, most of the people who filled the system were primarily Black and arrested on various unemployment charges. Thus, it can be easily argued that if the state focused on unemployment, and not racist arrests, there would have never been a need to build more prisons. Instead, PIRA and the racially charged labor system, cleared the path for Black families to be destroyed by the prison system for the next 100 years.

The very idea of convict leasing stemmed from an 1871 court ruling from Ruffin v. Commonwealth of Virginia that set the precedent for state control of inmate bodies and labor:

> *"For the time, during his term of service in the penitentiary, he is in a state of penal servitude to the State. He has, as a consequence of his crime, not only forfeited his liberty but all his personal rights except those which the law in its humanity accords to him. He is for the time being a slave of the State. He is civiliter mortus; and his estate, if he has any, is administered like that of a dead man."*

DC has historically been a central location for private prison operations. From 1820 to 1850, slave traffickers travelled through DC to detain slaves.

Opposition to the domestic slave trade in DC can be traced as far back as 1802. By 1807, President Thomas Jefferson, signed a law making it illegal to

---

55 Douglas A. Blackmon, *Slavery by Another Name: The Re-enslavement of Black Americans from the Civil War to World War 2* (New York, New York: Anchor Books, 2008)

import slaves into the United States. Criticizing slave commerce in the nation's capital became the cornerstone of the abolitionist movement.

According to the British and Foreign Anti-Slavery Society, "more extensive slave-dealers had private prisons throughout DC." An 1841 volume states that these "places of deposit are strongly built, and well supplied with thumbscrews and gags, and ornamented with cowskins and other whips, oftentimes bloody."[56]

In 1816, a woman named Anna jumped from the third floor of a well-known prison in DC, George Miller's Tavern; inspiring Representative John Randolph of Virginia to make the first Congressional indictment of the domestic slave trade – and the private prisons that made it possible calling for an investigation of the "inhuman and illegal traffic in slaves carried in and though the District."

During a renewed push to end slavery in 1848, Representative John Crowell of Ohio exposed one of the private prisons he was familiar with near the Smithsonian Institute on the National Mall, declaring that the museum focus was to educate people but doubted that it would be providing education on the prison that was near it. Two years later, in 1850, Congress passed a law to make slavery illegal in DC; eventually leading to the 13th Amendment.

This mishandled transition from slavery to industry, forced vulnerable slaves into new labor arrangements that left them deeply depressed, eventually pushing them outside the labor market. Fortunately, this would soon lead to the first Black millionaires and the creation of Black Wall Street.

By 2000, prison slavery had taken on a life of its own. That year one of the largest slave plantations in North Carolina was purchased for a contract with Wackenhut Corrections Corporation to build a new correctional facility. After construction, 1,200 prisoners from Washington, DC were transferred to the old Vann plantation to serve their sentences.

There was a book written by Si Kahn and Elizabeth Minnich, *The Fox in the Henhouse*, that focused on the level of cruelty the state had to exude to send

---

56  The slave-trade roots of US private prisons https://www.pri.org/stories/2016-08-26/slave-trade-roots-us-private-prisons

more than 1,000 Blacks to a former plantation as inmates. In their book, they state "so a for-profit corporation is importing well over one thousand Black men from the District of Columbia and imprisoning them on the same plantation where other African Americans, possibly including some of their own ances- tors, were held as slaves 150 years ago."[57]

In 2016, President Obama announced that the United States will no longer accept private prisons. This led to the closing of numerous prisons across the country with the agreement that when the last private prison contracts lapse in 2021, officials promise to let those contracts expire. However, the next year, in 2017, Trump, eradicated this measure; re-opening the flood gates for convict leasing.

The echoes of slavery still ring loud throughout the prison system. With rural areas being stifled by a downward spiral of manufacturing and skilled jobs, the corrections industry continues to thrive as the new workforce plan. This role makes it increasingly difficult for states to support humanity rather than health or even possibly, freedom. Nevertheless, this makes the cause of prison reform even more critical now than ever as the physical and psychologi- cal landscapes of the prisons are being reimagined. Understanding the history of slavery and its direct connection to the prison system will help in forming current efforts for prison reform.

# Ellen and William Craft (1824 – 1900; 1826 – 1891)

Abolitionists, Fugitive Slaves

Ellen Craft was born into slavery in 1824 in Clinton, Georgia to her slave moth- er and white owner. Having very fair skin, she was often mistaken for a member of her owner's white family. As a pre-teen, she was given away as a wedding gift to be sent to Georgia. William Craft, also born a slave in 1826, was later sold to pay off his master's gambling debt.

---

57 The slave-trade roots of US private prisons https://www.pri.org/stories/2016-08-26/slave-trade- roots-us-private-prisons

Meeting in Macon, GA, the couple decided to get married in 1846. However, they were not allowed to live together since they had separate owners. Growing in pain from the distance, they soon started to develop an escape plan, saving any money they could earn.

In December of 1848, the couple escaped slavery. Using her light skin to her advantage, Ellen dressed as a white man and claimed her husband was her slave. Amazingly, the plan worked and the couple settled in Boston, MA. The story of their romantic escape grew national attention and fame.

Sharing their story helped to generate considerable wealth for the family. Taking those funds, the Crafts started a furniture business and became abolitionists. They also toured with William Wells Brown to host antislavery lectures.[58]

When Congress passed the Fugitive Slave Act in 1850, two slave catchers traveled to Boston to return the Crafts. In an interesting turn of events, the town of Boston hid the couple and kept the bounty hunters from getting close to them.

Nevertheless, no longer feeling safe in America, the Crafts moved to England in 1851 and settled in West London where they became even more famous during the British abolitionist movement. By 1860, they published and depicted their escape in Running a Thousand Miles for Freedom.

They raised five children, became teachers and managed a boardinghouse. Expanding even further, William established commercial agreements in West Africa.

After the Emancipation Proclamation and having lived in England for 19 years, the Crafts returned to America in 1870. They landed in Savannah, GA and started the Woodville Cooperative Farm School in 1873 to educate the newly freed slaves.

With short lived success, the school closed due to lack of funding and the Crafts lost their farm due to the significant drop in the price of cotton in the mid-1880s. In 1890, the couple went to live with their daughter in Charleston. Ellen passed in 1891 with William Craft joining her in 1900.

---

58  Ellen and William Craft http://www.blackpast.org/aah/craft-william-and-ellen-1824-1900-1826-1891

# Frederick Hutson

Founder, Pigeonly

*Redefining imprisonment*

Frederick Hutson is a man who sees business opportunities in everything. By his own admission, this doesn't always work out for the best. Hutson spent over four years in prison after getting busted for an opportunity he saw in drug trafficking, a huge market, and one that was as he saw it, ripe for disruption. Police busted him at his Vegas mail store, where he'd been reducing inefficiencies by rerouting marijuana through his Florida business via FedEx, UPS and DHL.

Hutson, who'd built several businesses before and after a stint in the Air Force, which he left with an honorable discharge, began meditating on new ideas soon after he started his 51-month sentence in 2007, aged 24. "I did my time that way," he says. "While I was there I just saw how grossly inefficient the prison system was and there was just so many opportunities."

A big gripe for the 2.3 million doing time in the US is keeping in touch with friends and family on the outside. There's no internet in prison so all communication is through snail mail or the phone. Calls are often expensive and long distance. Relatives and friends, leading increasingly digitized lives, write less and don't get around to sending photos for weeks on end.

"It was a pain point I experienced firsthand," says Hutson. "I'm very close with my family and I knew they cared about me but even with knowing how much they cared about me they were still sometimes unable to send me photos."

Transitioning from digital to analog is tough, says Hutson. It's hard to sit down and write a letter now but simple to text or email. What if you created a website that printed out emails, texts or photos from your computer, Facebook or Instagram and mailed them for you in the plain white envelopes these institutions favored?

The idea for Pigeonly was born. Essentially, it's a platform that centralizes the myriad state-level databases making it a quick search to find where an

inmate is in the system - Hutson himself was moved eight times during his stay —
as well as a way to communicate. "People get lost in the system all the time," he
explains. "We have attorneys contacting us trying to find their clients."

*Extracted from Hollie Slade, Forbes*

# Black Wall Street (1921)

*In 1911, the Black dollar was worth over $700 million*

IT MAY NOT be surprising to learn that the Jackson Ward neighborhood of Richmond is the birthplace of Black capitalism and formerly known as the original Black Wall Street. During the early 1900s it was one of the wealthiest Black communities in America. This neighborhood boosted theaters, stores and medical facilities. Duke Ellington and Louis Armstrong visited the town, staying at the Eggleston Hotel, one of the few upscale hotels for Blacks in the south.

During 1888-1929, Richmond held six Black-owned banks, growing to lead the nation at 14 in 1914. The United Order of True Reformers was headquartered in Richmond. In the 1900s this was considered one of the most powerful Black fraternal and entrepreneurship organizations in the country. In 1888, they made history by forming the first bank to be chartered by Blacks in America. The True Reformers membership grew above 100,000 and would help spawn people such as Madame C. J. Walker; Maggie Walker, Emmet Burke, and the St. Luke Penny Savings Bank; John Mitchell Jr. and the Mechanics Savings Bank; Southern Aid, the Richmond Beneficial Insurance Company; and North Carolina Mutual.

The Black education and religious institutions were essential to Richmond's growth and the success of the early Black renaissance. Generation after generation was groomed by successful entrepreneurs that lead family businesses that pre-dated the Civil War.

The first Black man allowed to make a professional presentation to whites on a grand stage, Booker T. Washington was a notable business man amongst his multitude of accomplishments and in 1907 he wrote "The Negro in Business."

When reflecting on Booker T.'s history, his business acumen and authorship of an economics book is often downplayed or not mentioned.

In 1911, the Black dollar was worth over $700 million. By 1917, Blacks owned and operated more than 200 types of businesses. The 1912 "Negro Yearbook" indicates that Blacks owned "bakeries, shoe repair, dressmaking, fishing, sail making, medical services, legal service, and funeral home businesses[59]."

Founded in 1910, the National Urban League (NUL) is an historic civil rights organization dedicated to the economic empowerment in underserved communities. It is headquartered in New York City and spearheads the efforts of local affiliates through the development of programs, public policy research and advocacy. Today there are more than 100 affiliates in 36 states and DC, providing direct impact on the lives of more than 2 million people.

In 1915, William Latham, an attorney from Jackson, Mississippi, founded the Chicago Insurance Company – now, Underwriters Insurance Company. Jesse Binga, also in Chicago, controlled large amounts of real estate and banking.

Herman Perry of Standard Life, a Black legal reserve company, was also the owner of Penny Savings Bank of Augusta, Georgia, Service Farm Bureau, Service Laundry and Citizen Discount Corporation.

Born in Jamaica and arriving from New York City in 1916, Marcus Garvey, founded the Universal Negro Improvement Association, with the purpose of urging Black workers to be ready when the opportunity arose to leave the country. He firmly supported Black professionals in pursuit of financial empowerment.

With a surge of racial pride and income, Blacks began transitioning into being consumers. It is estimated that the 2017 buying power of Blacks is $1.3 trillion. Clothes and car purchases are suffocating the community. They provide no appreciation or return on investment. Blacks represent 25% of all suit buyers and 10% of all car consumers.

Maggie Lena Walker, school teacher and daughter of a freed slave, was the first Black woman to charter a bank - St. Luke Penny Savings Bank was founded in 1903. It provided loans to those who were denied by traditional banks.

---

59 History of Black Economic Empowerment https://www.deomi.org/downloadableFiles/Black_History_Month_2010.pdf

Interestingly, these would be Black lawyers, doctors and entrepreneurs more frequently than not.

Eventually a few of the Black banks decided to merge under the name Consolidated Bank and Trust. By the end of the 1900s, it was the last Black-owned bank in Richmond and was struggling to raise capital. In 2005, a Washington, DC bank bought it, followed by a bank from West Virginia in 2011 who then renamed it Premier Bank, placing a casket on the last bank of Black Wall Street. Premier Bank remains in the same location where Consolidated once stood.

In 1907, Oklahoma was made a state. It grew a reputation for change and acceptance so many Blacks began to travel there for a safe-haven. Most came by wagon and some even walked. Interestingly, "a huge portion of Blacks who went to Oklahoma had predecessors who could be followed back to Oklahoma. A large portion of the pilgrims were relatives of Blacks who had gone by walking with the Five Civilized Tribes along the Trail of Tears. Others were the relatives of Blacks who had fled to Native American Territory."[60] Many Blacks were from the Muskogee-talking people, such as Creeks, Seminoles, and the Yuchi.

"Senate Bill Number 1, the state's first piece of legislation, prevented coloreds from residing, traveling and marrying outside their race."[61]

It is noted that the Greenwood neighborhood of Tulsa, Oklahoma reached unprecedented economic levels compared to other communities during segregation. Most residents viewed Tulsa as two separate towns that contained Blacks north of the Frisco railroad tracks. They named this area "Little Africa." By 1921 it was home to 10,000 Blacks.

Greenwood focused on a road known as Greenwood Avenue that ran north for over a mile from the Frisco Railroad yards, and it was one of only a few avenues that did not cross through both neighborhoods.

Black business visionary, J. B. Stradford arrived in Tulsa in 1899, realizing that Blacks could hold a superior stance over the whites if resources were pooled. He purchased land in the northeast section of Tulsa, divided it up and

---

60 The O.W. Gurley Story https://www.linkedin.com/pulse/ow-gurley-story-former-president-grover-cleveland-appointee-golden

61 Black Wall Street http://www.blackwallstreet.org/owgurly

only sold to Blacks. O.W. Gurley, a wealthy Black from Arkansas, later moved to Tulsa in 1906 and purchased over 40 acres of land that he only sold to other Blacks. This created a refuge for Blacks looking to escape Mississippi.

Gurley, Stradford and other businessmen called The Founding Fathers of Black Economics, soon joined together on the same mission — buying and providing land for Blacks. Stradford created the famous Stradford Hotel on Greenwood, allowing Blacks to enjoy a downtown hotel where only whites are usually served. It was the largest owned Black Hotel in the country.

During her 1910 national tour, Madame C. J. Walker visited Greenwood. By 1917, she became the first Black millionaire, producing hair care products for women and men. Other notable producers made dyes, soaps, radios, burial caskets, coal, dolls, food and personal goods.

While there were only two airports in the state of Oklahoma, six Black families owned their own planes. The average income for a Tulsa Black family in 1910 ran up to $500 a day, well exceeding today's average — without even adjusting for inflation!

Money circulated 36 to 100 times in this small community. A single dollar would stay in Tulsa for almost a year before leaving the Black community. According to a 2014 report by the NAACP, "a dollar can circulate in Asian communities for a month, Jewish communities for 20 days and white communities for 17, but it now leaves the modern-day Black community in six hours."[62]

The event that led to the Tulsa riot on June 1, 1921 was the arrest of a Black man, Dick Rowland. On May 31st, the Tulsa Tribune reported an alleged assault by Rowland against Sara Page, a white female. There was never any evidence for the allegations against Rowland, yet white citizens began to gather at the courthouse where Rowland was being held with threats of lynching him.

Later that day, roughly 75 armed Blacks came to the courthouse to protect Rowland after learning that the group of whites were growing. When they arrived, a fight quickly started and a shot was fired. As Blacks attempted to retreat, they were followed by whites back into their neighborhoods. With whites breaking into stores for guns and receiving them from police officers, they

---

62 6 Interesting Things You Didn't Know About Black Wall Street. http://atlantablackstar.com/2014/12/02/6-interesting-things-you-didnt-know-about-black-wall-street/2/

became armed fast. With the number of whites exceeding Blacks, battles soon became plummets. By the end of June 1, the burgeoning Black community of Tulsa, Oklahoma had been destroyed.

"Many accounts of the demise of Black Wall Street refer to it as a race riot, but nothing could be further from the truth. It is better described as a terrorist attack on an affluent Black neighborhood."[63]

Rich in oil, Oklahoma, offered Blacks the chance to escape the South. In Tulsa, the railroad tracks separated the white part of town from the Greenwood District known as Little Africa. At the time, there were laws preventing both whites and Blacks from living in neighborhoods where the population was 75% of one race, helping to ease segregation.

Lining Greenwood Avenue with red brick buildings that thrived from the 1910 oil boom, a Black middle class was forming and growing. The schools were even better than those in the white areas and most houses had indoor plumbing before the white areas. The community had two newspapers, the Tulsa Star and the Oklahoma Sun.

While the wealth was growing fast, the hate from the 2,000 KKK local members grew faster. With whites returning home as World War I unemployed veterans, tensions began to rise as jobs and financial security became scarce.

Nearly every business in all 35 blocks that formed the Greenwood neighborhood were torched to the ground and looted for private use. At least $1.8 million was lost in property - $30 million in today's terms. More than 800 people were admitted to the hospitals, with 9,000 left homeless. 1,256 residences were destroyed and 600 successful businesses were lost, including 21 restaurants, 30 grocery stores, two movie theatres and a hospital. The KKK riot lasted for 16 hours.

Bodies were placed in unmarked graves and dumped into the Arkansas River. It is estimated that 300 – 400 Blacks died. "Many of the survivors mentioned bodies were stacked like cord wood," says Richard Warner of the Tulsa Historical Society.

Even worse, 6,000 Blacks that survived but did not flee the city were placed under arrest and put into internment camps, for months in some cases. Those

63 Ever Heard of Black Wall Street http://progressive.org/dispatches/ever-heard-black-wall-street/

that could leave within a short period of arrival had to obtain permission from the government and demonstrate proof of employment. Those that could not meet those requirements were placed into forced labor, usually sanitation.

It wasn't until 1997, nearly eighty years after the riot, that a commission was formed to study exactly what occurred. It is suspected that Dick Rowland and Sara Page were actually lovers. On May 30, 1921 – Memorial Day – a scream was heard from Sara while they were together. Upon questioning, Sara denied that Dick assaulted or did anything to her. Nevertheless, the afternoon paper, the Tulsa Tribune, ran the headline "Nab Negro for Attacking Girl in an Elevator." The local police, helped to manufacture this article as they were aware of the ramifications – lynching of Dick Rowland.

The commission recommended reparation be paid to the direct survivors of the riot. While a memorial was placed near the affected area in 2001, reparations were never received. Alfred Brophy argues that reparations are necessary because "the city was culpable, there were survivors, the harm was concentrated in one time and place, and even at the time, some city leaders acknowledged moral responsibility by promising that they would rebuild what had been destroyed." This argument made it to the US Supreme Court in 2004, who ultimately decided not to consider the case, due to statute of limitations.

# O. W. Gurley (1868 – unknown)
The Visionary Builder and President Cleveland Appointee

O. W. Gurley was born in 1868 to two former slaves. He dreamt of being rich and having political power.

In 1906, Gurley moved to Tulsa, Oklahoma where he bought 40 sections of land "just to be sold to Blacks." This was a courageous, nearly impossible move at the time due to financial and political reasons.

Starting with a boarding house that was positioned on a dirt road close to the train tracks, this street was named Greenwod Avenue. He named it after a city in Mississippi as many Blacks came to that area to escape the harsh world of the 'sip. They found safety on Greenwood where racism was nearly forgotten. This community became known as Black Wall Street.

From there Gurley built three two-story buildings and five homes. Unbelievably, he then purchased an 80-section piece of land in Rogers County and founded what is known today as Vernon AME Church.

The lines that divided the isolated community of Greenwood still function today: "Pine Street toward the North, Archer Street and the Frisco tracks toward the South, Cincinnati Street on the West, and Lansing Street on the East."[64]

Since the racial tension kept Blacks from shopping anywhere but Greenwood, businesses began to fill the streets including law and doctor offices. Schools were erected named for Dunbar and Booker T. Washington. Other establishments include Mount Zion Baptist Church, Ricketts' Restaurant, The Williams Dreamland Theater, Mann's Grocery Stores, Stradford Hotel and a slew of drug stores, cafes, barbershops and beauty salons.

Sadly, Gurley's influence and wealth did not last long. During the Oklahoma riots that attacked Black Wall Street, O. W. Gurley lost $200,000. He then exiled himself to California and vanished from the history books. He was honored in Before They Die! The Road to Reparations, a 2008 documentary.

# Bjorn BK Simmons

Founder, Wyzerr
Community Catalyst, StartupCincy

*Building an urban tech community*

Bjorn Simmons is a 26-year old entrepreneur, activist, and co-founder of tech startup company Wyzerr. Bjorn is a first-generation graduate from University of Arkansas, where he received his BA in Marketing Management and Entrepreneurship at the Sam M. Walton College of Business. Bjorn is an emerging Renaissance Man with leadership experience across many fields.

---

64 The O. G. Gurley Story https://www.linkedin.com/pulse/ow-gurley-story-former-president-grover-cleveland-appointee-golden

He began his career in marketing working for Sam Club before relocating to the city of Atlanta, GA. There he became immersed into the world of politics serving as a Chief of Staff for the Georgia House of Representatives. Under the leadership of Democratic Leader Stacey Abrams and House Minority Whip Carolyn Hugley, Bjorn served multifaceted roles that required him to operate as a community activist, campaign manager, field director and special projects coordinator with the senior staff team, that became known as The Gladiators.

It wasn't long before his political tenacity extended back to his home state, where served as PR and Outreach Specialist in the Arkansas House of Representatives under Minority Leader Eddie Armstrong and Assistant Director of the Arkansas Voter Registration Project.

Wyzerr, his company, is joining the data revolution by turning long, boring surveys into interactive smartforms, optimized for mobile technology. Wyzerr Smartforms look and feel like games while collecting 25-35 data points in seconds. Wyzerr is currently scaling it operations at the Brandery Venture Accelerator Program in Cincinnati, Ohio Additionally, at StartupCincy, BK is focused on "collaborating with and amplifying the excitement of the entrepreneurial community. Bjorn will be a part of the grand mission to bring national attention to our region by quantifying the collective efforts of StartupCincy, curating events and experiences."[65]

---

65  Ramping Up with New Team Members http://www.cintrifuse.com/blog/new-mktg-members/

# Kingman Park (1947)

*"Only the finest Black families can buy there"*

— CHARLES SAGER

KINGMAN PARK, THE hidden jewel of DC, is the first neighborhood designed for Black affluent residents in the country. Named after Brigadier General Dan Chrisite Kingman, the former head of the US Army Corp of Engineers, Kingman Park was established in 1919 as parkland for the Anacostia Water Park. "In 1891, the Army Corp of Engineers convinced Congress to approve the dredging of the Anacostia River to create a more functional water way for commercial use, while using the dredged material to build up the mud flats to create dry land."[66]

In 1927, Charles Sager, a DC real estate developer, started building homes in Kingman Park. The first 40 homes were built on 24th Street NE and sold by July 1928. In 1931, Sagar started building another 350 homes, opening the sale of these houses to be potentially purchased by Blacks; making Kingman Park home of some of the first Black homeowners in the country.

Housed in Capitol Hill South, town is located within one mile of Stadium Armory Metro Station.

Beautiful, willow oak trees line the most prominent section of Kingman Park – 21st Street from D Street to Benning Rd, NE.

Comprised of about 60 acres and 40 square blocks, the community has a rough triangular shape pressed against an enclave on the Anacostia River. The look and feel of the area is that of a Washington suburb.

---

66 History of Kingman Park http://kingmanpark.com/history.html

Interestingly, Kingman Park was originally planned for whites but they did not buy. Thus, in 1930, Sager led a promotional campaign that indicated that "only the finest Black families can buy there."[67] He realized a huge market opportunity for the Black Affluent.

Over the years, Young Elementary School and Brown Junior High School was formed. These schools would later receive historic designation as some of the first schools in America to support the Black community. Since its formation, Kingman Park has remained a "close-knit Black middle class community."

The first Black millionaire in DC resided there along with other Black lawyers, doctors, dentists, business owners and government employees. The first and only golf course designed for Blacks in DC, Langston Golf Course was constructed for the neighborhood in 1939. It remained one of the few places Blacks could freely play golf until the 1950s.

A few original residents still live there such as John D. and Alberta Sistare's (Angel Rich's great-grand parents) family on the prime block of 21ˢᵗ Street. Today, Kingman Park holds 10,000 residents and growing. It is one of the last best kept secrets in DC with skyrocketing property values. In 2016, the Kingman Park Civic Association nominated Kingman Park neighborhood as a historic district to protect the community from new development.[68]

# Madam CJ Walker (1867 – 1919)
Civil Rights Activist, Philanthropist and Entrepreneur

Sarah Breedlove was born on December 23, 1867 on a cotton plantation near Delta, Louisiana to the newly freed slaves, Owen and Minerva. After experiencing the deaths of her parents due to unknown causes, Sarah became an orphan at the mere age of 7 and went to live with her older sister, Louvinia. Together, with Louvinia's husband, they moved to Vicksburg, Mississippi in 1877 where it is believed by some that Sarah became a maid and cotton picker.

---

67  In RFK Stadium's shadow, a varied mix of homes with a rich history

68  Proposed Kingman Park Historic District https://planning.dc.gov/publication/proposed-kingman-park-historic-district

Her environment was harsh, holding her in constant agony between her work and the mistreatment by her brother-in-law. To escape this torture, she married a man named Moses McWilliams and gave birth to a daughter on June 6, 1885 named A'Lelia.

Two years later, after Moses died, Sarah took her daughter to St. Louis where her brothers were established barbers. She worked as a washerwoman earning $1.50 a day. Most of her earnings were used to send her daughter to public school in the day and Sarah attended at night whenever she could. It is in this town that she would meet her second husband, Charles J. Walker, who had a job in advertising and would later support her hair care company.

During the 1890s, after developing a scalp disorder that made her lose most of her hair, Sarah started experimenting with mixing store-brought solutions with home remedies. By 1905, she moved to Denver, Colorado with a job offer from Annie Turnbo Malone, a successful, Black, hair care entrepreneur.

While in Denver, Charles began helping Sarah create advertisements for her own hair care treatment – under the name Madam C.J. Walker.

In 1907, the power couple started traveling the South and Southeast to promote her products and give lectures on the "Walker Method." This method involved using her pomade, brushing and a heated comb.

The following year, Madam CJ opened a factory and beauty school in Pittsburgh, and by 1910 moved it to Indianapolis as the Madam CJ Walker Manufacturing Company became increasingly successful, generating revenue that would be equivalent to millions in modern times.

The company boosted its ability to create products and train salesmen, cre-ating one of the first multi-level marketing companies in the country that would later be replicated by companies such as Avon and Mary Kay. These salesmen became known as 'Walker Agents' and were highly respected throughout the Black communities of America.

The agents held strong to Walker's legacy of 'cleanliness and loveliness' to push Black America forward. As a pioneer of business leadership in America, Walker organized her agents, formed clubs and hosted annual conferences where she provided generous incentives for good sales. Agents also received awards and compensation for helping the community with philanthropic and educational efforts.

As her company grew stronger, her marriage grew weaker. Unfortunately, in 1913, Madam CJ and Charles divorced. She took the opportunity to travel throughout Latin America and the Caribbean to promote her business. Her daughter, A'Lelia Walker ran the business during her overseas travels and helped purchase property for the company in Harlem, New York. When Madam CJ returned in 1916, she moved to her new home in Harlem.

In addition to her amazing hair care company, Madam CJ Walker founded philanthropies that included educational scholarships and contributions to the National Association for the Advancement of Colored People (NAACP) and the National Conference on Lynching (NCL) among other organizations to enhance the lives of Blacks.

Due to hypertension, Madam CJ Walker died on May 25, 1919, at age 51. She was at her home in Irvington, New York that she built for herself.

When she passed, she remained the only owner of her business, valued at more than $1 million. She is the first Black millionaire on record. The Guinness Book of Records also maintains that she is the "first woman to become a millionaire by her own achievements."[69]

Madam CJ left one-third of her estate to her daughter, A'LeLia Walker. Inheriting her mother's empire, the Madam CJ Walker Manufacturing Company, A'LeLia grew to fame as a businesswoman in her own right. In 2016, Madam Walker's great-granddaughter, A'LeLia, expanded the brand with a progression partnership with Shea Moisture. It was announced in 2016 at an annual conference hosted by Natalie Cofield of Walker's Legacy, an organization based in Texas that was inspired by Madam Walker to empower women.

Madam CJ Walker holds two National Historic Landmarks in the United States. Her home was designated immediately after her death; followed by The Walker Building, an arts center that she started in 1927. In 1998, a stamp was created

---

69  Eleven Facts You Didn't Know About Madam C.J. Walker https://newsone.com/1592885/first-african-american-millionaire-madam-cj-walker/

for Madam CJ Walker as part of the Black Heritage series at the United States Postal Service.

# Natalie Cofield
Founder, Walker's Legacy

Natalie Madeira Cofield is a millennial serial entrepreneur, diversity champion, and award-winning executive. Cofield began her career working three jobs in high school, attended college at age 16, started her first company at 26, and later went on to become a three-time CEO by age 30. Today, Cofield is the Founder & CEO of Walker's Legacy, Walker's Legacy Foundation and Urban Co-Lab.

Walker's Legacy, a Google partner firm, is an organization she created to inspire, equip and empower professional and enterprising women which boasts a network of more than 14,000 women and growing. The organization has been named by Inc Magazine as one of the '25 Companies Determined to See Women Succeed'. The global women in business collective, which currently operates in more than twenty cities across the country, also has an adjoined nonprofit arm, Walker's Legacy Foundation, funded by the W.K. Kellogg Foundation, which was founded in 2016.

Urban Co-Lab is a social impact and inclusion incubator in Austin, Texas which was awarded one of the Top 10 Co-Working Spaces in Austin by CultureMap within the first two weeks of its opening in 2015. The organization is noted for producing and publishing the first Startup Diversity Report for the City of Austin.

As an advocate, Cofield has served as the youngest person to testify before the US Senate Committee on Small Business & Entrepreneurship in 2009 and is a sought-after expert for government and corporations on topics of diversity and inclusion.

Her work has been featured in CNN, NY Times, Inc, Fast Company, Forbes, Business Insider, Black Enterprise, Essence and Ebony among others. She has been the cover story of both Black Enterprise and Austin Woman. In 2015 Cofield was named one of the 100 Most Influential African Americans in the America by The Root 100. In 2013, Cofield was named the Technology Diversity Evangelist of the Year by Google and one of the Top 10 Black Innovators by MVMT50, an initiative of South by Southwest. In 2013, she was featured on the cover of Black Enterprise, in 2015 she was featured on the cover of Austin Woman Magazine. In 2016 Cofield was selected as an Ashoka Changemaker Fellow by Ashoka.

Cofield is an honors graduate of Howard University, where she was in the inaugural class of the Bill Gates Millennium Scholars Program and the Baruch School of Public Affairs. Cofield has spoken for global technology companies including IBM, Dell, Applied Materials, Google, and Facebook among others.

# Little Rock 9 (1957)

*In 1860, 90% of Blacks were slaves. Barely
10% learned to read and write.*

IN A HISTORIC and momentous event that changed the world, nine Black teenagers entered an all-white school in the south — as students. It was an unprecedented event that took place at Central High School in Little Rock, Arkansas in September 1957.

This landmark accomplishment was the result of a long arduous road for Blacks fighting for equal education and the direct implication of the US Supreme Court ruling segregation in public schools as unconstitutional in 1954 during the Brown v. Board of Education case in Topeka.

Not accepting or abiding by the court's decision, the Governor of Arkansas, Orval Faubus, requested the National Guard to block all Black students from entering the school. After withstanding daily attacks and pleading for help from the NAACP, the teens were finally provided some breathing room when President Eisenhower sent in federal troops to escort the Little Rock Nine into the school. This decision forever changed the landscape of not just Black America or even America, but the world.

Understanding that Black literacy would threaten the economy of slavery — which relied on slaves being dependent to their masters — Blacks were previously forbidden by law to learn how to read and write. Most whites felt that an educated slave would threaten their authority. It was an actual crime for Blacks to be educated.

Black literacy was a serious threat to the Deep South. Anyone taught teaching a slave how to read was ran out of the state. In Norfolk, Virginia,

Margaret Douglas was caught teaching Black children and was imprisoned for her actions.[70]

## *Excerpt from South Carolina Act of 1740*

Whereas, the having slaves taught to write, or suffering them to be employed in writing, may be attended with great inconveniences; Be it enacted, that all and every person and persons whatsoever, who shall hereafter teach or cause any slave or slaves to be taught to write, or shall use or employ any slave as a scribe, in any manner of writing whatsoever, hereafter taught to write, every such person or persons shall, for every such offense, forfeit the sum on one hundred pounds, current money.

## *Excerpt from Virginia Revised Code of 1819*

That all meetings or assemblages of slaves, or free negroes or mulattoes mixing and associating with such slaves at any meeting-house or house, and in the night; or at any school or schools for teaching reading or writing, either in the day or night, under whatsoever pretext, shall be deemed and considered an unlawful assembly; and any justice of a county, and wherein such assemblage shall be, either from his own knowledge or the information of others, of such unlawful assemblage and may issue his warrant, directed to any sworn officer or officers, authorizing him or them to enter the house houses where such unlawful assemblages and may be for the purpose of apprehending or dispersing such slaves, and to inflict corporal punishment on the offender or offenders, at the discretion of any justice of the peace, not exceeding twenty lashes.[71]

In his book, *Narrative of the Life and Adventures of Henry Bibb, An American Slave*, Henry Bibb stated "Slaves were not allowed books, pen, ink, nor paper, to improve their minds. There was a Miss Davies, a poor white girl, who offered to

---

70  Education of Slaves http://spartacus-educational.com/USASeducation.htm

71  Education, Arts and Culture http://www.pbs.org/wnet/slavery/experience/education/docs1.html

teach Sabbath School for the slaves. Books were supplied and she started the school; but the news got to our owners that she was teaching us to read. This caused quite an excitement in the neighborhood. Patrols were appointed to go and break it up the next Sabbath."

The first African Free School opened in New York City in 1787 with the mission of educating Blacks to be equal to whites. Starting as a one-room schoolhouse with 40 students, the school along with 6 others eventually began receiving public funding in 1824.

In Canterbury, Connecticut a Quaker named Prudence Crandall opened a school for Black girls. When the local whites found out they attempted to burn down the school and soon began using vagrancy laws or Black Codes against them. The girls became legally entitled to 10 lashes if caught attending the school. William Lloyd Garrison reported the case in *The Liberator* with the support of the Anti-Slavery Society.

While in 1849 Charles Summer lost his case when helping Sarah Roberts to sue Boston for not admitting Blacks to its school, in 1855 the Massachusetts Legislature altered its policy to declare that "no person shall be excluded from a Public School on account of race, color or prejudice."

Creating a school for Blacks in Andersonville, Mary Battey wrote in 1866 "our school begun – in spite of threatenings from the whites, and the consequent fear of the Blacks – with twenty-seven pupils, four only of whom could read, even the simplest words. At the end of six weeks, we have enrolled eighty-five names, with but fifteen unable to read. In seven years teaching at the North, I have not seen a parallel to their appetite for learning, and their active progress… Their spirit now may be estimated somewhat, when I tell you that three walk a distance of four miles, each morning, to return after the five-hour session. Several come three miles, and quite a number from two and two-and-a-half miles."

In 1860, 90% of Blacks were slaves. Barely 10% learned to read and write. The literacy gap between blacks and whites born between 1800 and 1860 was 70 percentage points. Today it still exceeds 40 points in some urban areas.

The disenfranchisement of Blacks enabled administrators to easily build quality white schools at the expense of Black ones. The incentives for investing in education were strong. Resources for Black schools began to expand about 20 years before the Supreme Court's Brown v. Board decision, but it was not until the late 1960s that southern schools started to really desegregate.

# Mary McLeod Bethune (1875 – 1955)
Civil Rights Activist, Educator

Mary Jane McLeod was born on July 10, 1875 in Mayesville, South Carolina as one of 17 children of former slaves in poverty. All the family members worked with most picking cotton for a living. Mary was the only child in the family to go to school. She walked several miles back and forth each day to the local Black school. She studied extremely hard and shared her knowledge with her family.

She received a scholarship to an all-girls school in Scotia Seminary in Concord, North Carolina. Graduating in 1893, she then attended the Dwight Moody's Institute for Home and Foreign Missions – Moody Bible Institute – in Chicago. After graduating two years later, she returned to the South and became a teacher.

In 1898, she married Albertus Bethune. Together they had one son, Albert Bethune, before divorcing in 1907.

During her marriage, she founded the Daytona Normal and Industrial Institute for Negro Girls in Daytona, Florida, in 1904. She took charge as the President of the school. Budding from five students, her school grew to exceed 250 students at a rapid pace. In 1923, the school merged with the Cookman Institute for Men and was renamed Bethune-Cookman College, now a Historically Black College. She remained the leader, providing one of the few places that Blacks could achieve higher learning, until 1942.

After serving as President of the Florida chapter, Mary became the National President of the National Association of Colored Women in 1924. She beat out fellow reformer "Ida B. Wells for the top post."[72]

She gained a steep influence on government affairs and was invited by President Coolidge to a conference on child welfare. She later served on the Commission on Home Building and Home Ownership for President Hoover.

---

72  Mary McLeod Bethune http://www.biography.com/people/mary-mcleod-bethune-9211266

By 1935, she was a special advisor on minority affairs for President Roosevelt. That year, she started her own organization, the National Council of Negro Women. The next year, Roosevelt promoted her to Director of Negro Affairs of the National Youth Administration to help young people find job opportunities. Most importantly, she became a trusted friend to the President as well as his wife.

She settled the headquarters of the National Council of Negro Women in Washington, DC in 1943. The rowhouse also served as her residence. As a founding member of the NAACP, she represented the organization with W.E.B. DuBois in 1945.

President Truman appointed her to a committee on national defense and to serve as an official delegate in Liberia. Her memoirs, My Last Will and Testament, provided an inner perspective on her life and legacy. She closed them with "If I have a legacy to leave my people, it is my philosophy of living and serving."

Getting older, Mary returned to Florida to retire and later passed on May 18, 1955. In 1973, Mary McLeod Bethune was inducted into the National Women's Hall of Fame and she was issued a US Postal stamp in her honor in 1985. The NCNW former headquarters is now the Mary McLeod Bethune House National Historic Site.

# Stacie Whisonant
Founder, GO Pay Your Tuition

Stacie Whisonant was lucky. The military paid for her college education. She served for eight years in the Army. Her sister was not so lucky. She paid for college herself. Because Whisonant wasn't burdened by debt, she was able to buy a house. Her sister had to pay off student loans.

Whisonant saw an opportunity to serve the 60% to 70% of students who are getting turned down for student loans because a parent can't afford to be a cosigner. The turndown market is $250 billion, she noted.

Whisonant started PYT Funds ("Pay Your Tuition") to tackle the growing college loan funding gap. '[Financial] resources are available for freshman and sophomores but taper off as college students near graduation," says Whisonant. Students who can't find funding don't graduate and are still saddled with paying off student loans from earlier years.

Using a combination of crowdfunding, philanthropy and data science, PYT helps high-performing low- and moderate-income college students get the funding they need to finish college. Its KYS ("Know Your Student") proprietary process allows PYT to provide a more transparent and predictive lending solution with low default rates based on a more comprehensive understanding of its students than that of any traditional FICO lender. Academic (such as grades), social (such as internships while at school) and professional (building networks and relationships) data are included in the algorithm. Lending institutions expand their consumer loan portfolio by funding lower-risk private education loans.

Students ask for $25 to $50 donations from friends and family. The $1,000 to $2,000 raised serves as collateral for getting a $5,000 loan. For those that can't raise that amount of money, Whisonant has formed a foundation to provide funding.

*Extracted from Geri Stengel, Forbes*

# Banking Black (1968)

*"I call upon you to take your money out of the banks downtown
and deposit your money in the Tri-State Bank"*

— DR. MARTIN LUTHER KING

IN MEMPHIS, TENNESSEE on April 3, 1968, Martin Luther King Jr. delivered his famous "I've Been to the Mountaintop" speech. In the speech, he asked Blacks to #BankBlack, meaning to put their money in Black-owned banks. Specifically, King said "we've got to strengthen Black institutions. I call upon you to take your money out of the banks downtown and deposit your money in the Tri-State Bank. We want a bank-in movement in Memphis... We begin the process of building a greater economic base."

King was assassinated the next day. His hopes of increasing Black wealth died along with him. Blacks commonly relied on Black community banks in cities such as Chicago, Atlanta, Richmond, and DC for providing loans as well as boosting Black churches, businesses, and ultimately neighborhoods during segregation. After desegregation, money began to flow from Black to White-owned banks, decreasing the value of Black communities.

According to Michael Grant, president of the National Bankers Association, representing 200 minority and women-owned banks there was a "toxic side" to integration. He says, "the financial meltdown of 2007 wiped out 40% of Black wealth in the United States, killing off many of these already struggling community banks" that were not part of the Wall Street bailout. Just 25 Black owned banks remain in America, according to a 2016 FDIC report, compared with 45 10 years ago. Grant states that at the peak of the banking Black movement, there were more than 100.

"Racial bias in the lending industry remains all too common, despite legislation aimed at preventing it. In 1992, a landmark study from the Federal Reserve Bank of Boston examined 4,500 mortgage-loan applications and discovered that Black borrowers were twice as likely to get rejected for loans as white borrowers with similar credit histories. More recently, an economics professor at the University of Massachusetts found that banks in Boston and across the state of Massachusetts continue to reject Black and Latino borrowers for home mortgages at a much higher rate than whites.[73]

In fact, the Consumer Financial Protection Bureau (CFPB) is now sending undercover employees into banks across the country as potential homebuyers. In 2016, the CFPB sued BancorpSouth Bank in Mississippi for allegedly discriminating against Blacks. In this specific situation, the CFPB sent Black and white employees to the bank to apply for a home loan. The Black person, who had better credit, was allegedly steered toward a smaller loan with a higher interest rate.

In the wake of the Black Lives Matter movement, some Black banks have seen a recent surge in new bank accounts. Rapper Killer Mike asked Blacks on BET and MTV to put some of their money in Black banks, creating the hashtag #bankblack. This call to action led to Citizens Trust Bank, the only Black bank remaining in Atlanta, receiving 8,000 new applications a few days after his request.

In 1927, Major R. R. Wright and C. C. Spaulding formed the Negro Bankers Association, the first professional organization for Blacks in finance. In 1948, the organization changed its name to National Bankers Association and still exist today.

In 1970, Joseph Searless III became the first Black member of the New York Stock Exchange. That same year economist, university president, and corporate executive, Clifton Wharton Jr. served as Secretary of State during the Clinton Administration, assisted Rockefeller on Latin American economic development

---

73 The Rise and Fall of Black Wall Street. The Atlantic. https://www.theatlantic.com/business/archive/2016/08/the-end-of-black-wall-street/498074/

and became the first Black president of Michigan State University. In 1978, Wharton became the President of the State University of New York and by 1987 he became CEO of TIAA-CREFF, making him the first Black Chairman and CEO of a major US corporation.

By 1993, Harry Alford and Kay Debow founded the National Black Chamber of Commerce.

# Congressman Ron Dellums
Civil Rights Activist, Representative

Ronald Dellums was born on November 24, 1935 in Oakland, California to Verney and Willa Dellums. His uncle, C.L. Dellums, was a leader in the Brotherhood of Sleeping Car Porters union and was a major role model to him. He graduated from Oakland Technical High School in 1953.

The following year he enrolled in the Marine Corps. During his service, he married Athurine and had two children. They later divorced. In 1958, he earned an associate's degree and two years later graduated with a Bachelor of Arts from San Francisco State College. Two years after that he was awarded a master's degree in social work from the University of California at Berkeley.

In 1962, he married Leola Roscoe Higgs and they had three children together. In 1999, they divorced and he married Cynthia Lewis the following year.

Ron began his career as a psychiatric social worker for the California department of mental hygiene from 1962 to 1964. In 1967, he made his first step into politics when won a seat on the Berkeley city council. When asked to describe his political approach, he replied "I'd listen and try to understand what people had to say, but then I'd act on my own beliefs. That's the only way anyone should run for office."[74]

By 1970, he started a campaign for the congressional seat, competing against six-time incumbent, Jeffrey Cohelan. In 1971, he won 57% of the vote to become the first Black to represent a majority-white congressional district.

---

74  Ron Dellums http://history.house.gov/People/Listing/D/DELLUMS,-Ronald-V--(D000222)/

During the 92$^{nd}$ Congress, as a freshman member, Dellums introduced more than 200 pieces of legislation. "He displayed little patience for congressional customs and the inner workings of the institution. After the House refused to conduct an investigation on possible American war crimes in Vietnam, he spearheaded a plan to hold his own ad hoc hearings – an unusual and controversial move that provoked scorn from some longtime politicians but drew considerable media attention."[75]

"I am not going to back away from being called a radical. If being an advocate of peace, justice, and humanity toward all human beings is radical, then I'm glad to be called a radical." Dellums exclaimed during his first term.

He introduced extensive financial sanctions in South Africa as the first legislator to suggest such harsh restrictions against the apartheid regime. Dellums served as one of the 13 founding members of the Congressional Black Caucus (CBC) in 1971. With their support, he set forth on a long-term battle to reduce discrimination in South Africa. In 1972, Dellums stated "we are serious in our determination that positive action be taken soon to terminate US business relationships with apartheid and repression in Africa."

Eventually Dellums was arrested at the South African Embassy in Washington, DC.

1986 brought Dellums his greatest achievement. While William Gray III of Pennsylvania, a Black member, had introduced a bill calling for a US trade embargo on South Africa and divestment of American companies, Dellums produced a similar bill that was presented with lighter terms.

Unique to this moment, the opposing side did not request a recorded roll call vote after a voice vote passed Dellum's measure. He was shocked at the ease in which it passed and called it the highest point of his political life and the most rewarding. "It's been a long journey to this moment" Dellums stated with relief. On October 2, 1986, the Comprehensive Anti-Apartheid Act became law.

Another one of his goals was to cut the military budget. He rose through the ranks of Armed Services, and served for the rest of his House career, becoming chairman of the Subcommittee on Military Installations and Facilities in 1983.

---

75  Ron Dellums http://history.house.gov/People/Listing/D/DELLUMS,-Ronald-V--(D000222)/

10 years later he made history as the first Black Chairman of Armed Services. After holding the seat for one term, he became Ranking Member in 1995.

Averaging more than 60% of the vote for most of his career, Dellums seldom faced re-election issues. In February 1998, the 14-term Representative decided to resign from the House for personal reasons. He left with the words "to get up every day and put on your uniform and put on your tie and march on the floor of Congress knowing that, in your hands, in that card, in your very being, you have life and death in your hands, it is an incredible thing."

After leaving, he started his own firm and was elected Mayor of Oakland in 2006.

# Dominique Broadway

Founder, Finances Demystified
Co-Founder, The Modern Brown Woman

Provocateur and trailblazer can be used to describe this millennial. Dominique has transformed the reputation of personal finances into a social experience by making it engaging, trendy and easy to understand.

Dominique Broadway is an award winning Financial Planner, Personal Finance Coach, Speaker, Finance Expert, Entrepreneur and the Founder of Finances De•mys•ti•fied & The Social Money Tour. She has a strong passion for working with young professionals, entrepreneurs and people of all ages to bring their Dreams2Reality. Dominique began working at major brokerage firms such as UBS Financial Services and Edelman Financial Services, at the ripe age of 21, focusing on clients with $10 million and up in investable assets.

Shortly after launching Finances De•mys•ti•fied, an award-winning organization that provides Personal Finance Coaching & Financial Capability solutions, she was named one of the top Financial Advisors in the United States for Millennials, at the age of 28.

Dominique is known for being highly favored to share her entrepreneur story, financial expertise and words of wisdom to universities such as Georgetown University, Howard University and University of Maryland, among others and corporations such as NBC Universal and numerous non-profits. Dominique has also received various accolades such as the Top 30 Under 30 in Washington DC, the DC Future Business Leader of America Businessperson of the Year and nominated for the Changemaker of the Year for her work with Financial Literacy.

Dominique is proud alum of Bowie State University where she received her Bachelors of Business Administration with a focus on Banking and Finance. To further her education, she went on to receive her Masters of Science in Financial Management from University of Maryland University College.

Dominique's demystified financial advice, has been highlighted on Yahoo!, Forbes, TheNest.com, Baltimore Sun, Black Enterprise, Marketwatch.com, Ebony Magazine, Levo League, SmartCEO, U.S. News, USA Today, Refinery 29 and other media outlets.

# Reparations (1989)

*"We simply think that Congress should take a look at the lingering effects of slavery so that we may get a deeper appreciation of them and reach some consensus about what the solutions may be."*

— JOHN CONYERS

REPARATIONS IS DEFINED as the making of amends for a wrong one has done, by paying money to or otherwise helping those who have been wronged. The idea of reparations for slavery suggest that there should be some form of payment provided to descendants of the Atlantic Slave Trade.

Congressman John Conyers was the first to propose a federal study of reparations in 1989. The bill was called the "Hr – Commission to Study Reparation Proposals for African Americans Act." He has continued to propose that bill every year since 1989, although it has yet to ever pass.

In 2016, Ta-Nehisi Coates, a prominent journalist for The Atlantic published the now famous article, *The Case for Reparations*. In the article, she discussed the psychological implications of slavery on current Black people and the long-lasting effects of the Jim Crow laws. She unashamedly detailed her disappointment with Congress not passing Conyers' bill.

That same year, a United Nations declared that the United States owes reparations to African Americans, as compensation for "the legacy of colonial history, enslavement, racial subordination and segregation, racial terrorism and racial inequality." They published a report titled Working Group of Experts on People of African Descent and strongly encouraged payment by the US Government. Although the panel made these recommendations, it does not actually require the US government to make payments and will probably have no actual impact.

A research study by the University of Connecticut, calculated the value of US slave labor in the 89 years from 1776 until the end of the Civil War. It considered the equivalent wages paid to laborers at the time, assuming an average of 12 hours of work a day, seven days a week. Thomas Craemer, the researcher, concluded that US slave labor would be valued at roughly $6 trillion today. That figure is equivalent to the 10-year cost of Donald Trump's tax plan and is significantly less than Bernie Sander's health-care plan.[76]

Craemer argues that the UK is responsible for slave reparations owed before US independence. The researcher also did not consider thefts, lynchings or other forms of discrimination that would have impacted slaves. He felt it would be best to focus on the "easily defined and indisputable example of economic injury."

As a German, Craemer finds it difficult to understand how the German government has been paying reparations to Nazi victims for 60 years for a point in time event, the Holocaust; but Blacks have barely received an official apology.

"Incidentally, an independent analysis by the nonpartisan Tax Foundation estimated Trump's proposed tax plan could cost the government as much as $5.9 trillion in foregone revenue over a decade." And this is a reduction from a $9.5 trillion plan that was proposed a year prior according to the nonpartisan Tax Policy Center. Craemer's study also found that 7 in 10 people believe that the disparities in US income are too stark.

The fight for reparations continues in 2017 and the bill has been updated as H.R. 40 – Commission to Study and Develop Reparation Proposals for African-Americans Act.

# Congressman John Conyers
Civil Rights Activist

John Conyers was born on May 16, 1929. His father was a union activist for the Black auto painters. He was raised in Northwest Detroit, Michigan

---

76 The cost of slavery reparations is now within the boundaries of the politically acceptable https://www.washingtonpost.com/news/wonk/wp/2016/09/29/the-cost-of-slavery-reparations-is-now-within-the-boundaries-of-the-politically-acceptable/?utm_term=.ec48ce185819

with a passion for music. He played the bass, piano, tenor saxophone and trombone.

The 1943 race riots in Detroit had a major impact on his life. Witnessing Blacks being pulled off streetcars and getting attacked sparked his political interest. He graduated in 1954 but his family could not afford college so his father helped him gain employment as a spot-welder at Lincoln auto plant. He soon became Director of his United Auto Workers local unit.

He started taking night classes to learn chemistry and physics at Detroit's Wayne State University. In 1942, he enrolled on a scholarship to major in civil engineering. In 1950, he enlisted in the US Army and during his training went to Washington to watch Congress in action. It was then that he thought to himself "I could do that!" He went on to win several military honors, spending much of his time in Korea.

After the army, he leveraged his Veteran status to continue his education. He switched to law and graduated from Wayne State in 1957. That same year, he passed the bar and founded the law firm of Conyers, Bell, and Townsend. In 1963, he served on the National Lawyers Committee for Civil Rights Under Law, spearheaded by President John F. Kennedy.

He became elected to represent Michigan's First Congressional District. He was a co-sponsor of the landmark Voting Rights Act of 1965 and he backed legislation to establish the Medicare program with President Lyndon Johnson.

In 1969, Conyers became a founding member of the Congressional Black Caucus and served as its senior leader for many years. During his first year in Congress, and after the Watergate scandal, he supported the impeachment of President Nixon. "He had earned the 13th spot on Nixon's notorious "enemies list" of political opponents."[77]

He also introduced a bill to require health warning labels on alcoholic beverages. This bill became law in 1988.

Important to the Civil Rights Movement and Convict Leasing, Conyers was one of the first Congressman to "urge a systematic study of the differing treatment Blacks and whites received at the hands of police, and the US Department

---

77 John Conyers http://www.encyclopedia.com/history/historians-and-chronicles/historians-miscellaneous-biographies/john-jr-conyers

of Justice launched a major national investigation of the issue partly in response to his concerns."[78]

After Reverend Dr. Martin Luther King Jr. was assassinated, Conyers introduced a bill to make King's birthday a holiday in 1968. Nearly 20 years later, it was passed into law in 1983.

Interestingly, in 1998 he participated in the impeachment of President Clinton for lying about his affair with Monica Lewinsky.

In 2000, Conyers solidified himself in history by leading the effort to request reparations to be paid to Blacks as compensation for forced labor during slavery. Conyers expressed his feelings in a magazine article for Ebony saying that the request was "not coming forward in an accusatory tone towards any citizens or their ancestors. We simply think that Congress should look at the lingering effects of slavery so that we may get a deeper appreciation of them and reach some consensus about what the solutions may be. The issue of reparations is not something beyond our understanding. It is a pretty fundamental issue if you look at it. I'm saying it's time we did."

Later in 2005, Conyers along with Representative Stephanie Tubbs Jones introduced the Voting Opportunity and Technology Enhancement and Rights (VOTER) Act to address racial voting discrepancies from the 2002 and 2004 elections. He also worked to help Haiti and continues to support global Civil Rights issues.

# Jason Green
Co-founder, SkillSmart

Jason Green is an entrepreneur, lawyer, and political strategist that has spent his career empowering individuals and communities. He cofounded and serves as vice president for business development of SkillSmart, a software company enabling job seekers to reach their employment potential.

---

78 John Conyers http://www.encyclopedia.com/history/historians-and-chronicles/historians-miscellaneous-biographies/john-jr-conyers

Green is also directing a documentary exploring the historic community of Quince Orchard, Maryland, and whether it is a transferable model of how diverse communities can and must come together to preserve history and shape the future.

Prior to these endeavors, Green served in several state and local political positions. Most recently, Green served for four years as Associate Counsel to President Obama, where he advised on legal, economic and domestic policy matters. Prior to joining the White House, Green served as the National Voter Registration Director for the Obama for America 2008 campaign.

Green, a graduate of Washington University in St. Louis and Yale Law School, co-chairs a regional task force addressing cybersecurity employment, sits on a number of local boards and committees, and is a Fellow at Docs in Progress.

# Black Billionaires
# (2001)

*Fortune's 2002 issue of America's 40 Richest*
*Under 40 included six Blacks*

THROUGHOUT THE 1990s Blacks found a silver glimpse of hope in the entertainment industry. Much of the financial success of Black culture in the 90s and 2000s can be attributed to revenue from music, sports and television.

During this same period, Blacks made several advances in finance. Franklin Raines became chairman and CEO of Fannie Mae in 1999. In 2001, Kenneth Chenault became CEO of American Express and Richard Parsons became CEO of AOL-Time Warner.

Seizing this critical moment in history and standing in the crossroads at the right place at the right time was Robert Johnson.

Born in 1946, Robert Johnson is the founder of Black Entertainment Television and RLJ Development. He is also the former majority owner of the Charlotte Bobcats, a NBA franchise. In 2001, he became the first Black billionaire and the first Black person to be listed on any of Forbes world's rich lists. Founding it from scratch in 1980, Johnson sold BET for $3 billion, two decades later to Viacom.

Much of his success is due to the songs, music videos, styles and personalities that BET produced from Black music entertainers and entrepreneurs.[79] BET

---

79 The Columbia Guide to African American History Since 1939 https://books.google.com/books?id=Y6yuwT54mA0C&pg=PA201&lpg=PA201&dq=history+black+billionaire&source=bl&ots=x00JSlZdnB&sig=lFwaFlR5DvpSY8qrZPVmr4s_q1Q&hl=en&sa=X&ved=0ahUKEwjok6W49YvTAhXIh1QKHcYiD2k4ChDoAQgfMAE#v=onepage&q=history%20black%20billionaire&f=false

was the first Black-owned television network, opening an international market for hip-hop music and culture. Emerging from rap music that resurrected in the Bronx during the 1970s from Caribbean influences, hip-hop, was the new "get out the hood" card.

The name hip hop derived from DJs introducing rap songs by scratching them on turntables, stopping, starting and repeating beats. Graffiti and break dancing contributed to the growing phenomenon. Oprah once said she knew hip hop was a permanent part of American culture when she saw it featured in a Pillsbury commercial.

Russell Simmons, who founded Def Jam Records in 1984, was a pioneer entrepreneur in the hip-hop industry. His company held some of the major rap artists, helping his company grow to the largest Black-owned music business. In 1992, he produced Def Comedy Jam, helping to produce some of the biggest comedians in the world, including Dave Chappelle and Martin Lawrence. He won a Tony Award in 2003 for his Broadway show Def Poetry Jam as the best theatrical event.

Russell also emerged with other hip-hop innovations such as Phat Fashions and the Rush Card. Both, opening doors for trillion dollar industries that still thrive today.

Sean "Puff Daddy" "P Diddy" Combs, also conquered the hip-hop music and fashion industry with his Sean John label. Daymond John helped revolutionize hip-hop clothing with his brand, FUBU, For Us By US, grossing earnings of $380 million in 2000.

Undoubtedly, entertainment became the major growth engine of the Black community during the new millennium. Fortune's 2002 issue of America's 40 Richest Under 40 included six Blacks, all from the sports and entertainment industries. – Michael Jordan, Percy Miller "Master P," Sean Combs "Diddy," Tiger Woods, Shaquille O'Neal and Will Smith. Earvin "Magic" Johnson, who was 43 at the time of the list, missed it but had easily accumulated $500 million from his movie theatres, restaurants, shopping malls, and athletic clubs.

While Blacks saw great success, only two still stood when Forbes released its 2002 list of the 400 Richest People in America – Robert Johnson and Oprah Winfrey.

Oprah is proudly the first Black female billionaire. To become the world's best friend, she focused on what she calls "Black girlfriend talk." Oprah remained

America's top talk-show host for 20 years, establishing an untouchable brand that would move mountains just by the sound of her voice. For nearly a decade she was named the world's most influential person and still carries great influence today. She is a media conglomerate with companies in the film, cable, TV and publishing industry.

Her book club literally saved the book industry as any of her recommendations would immediately become best sellers. In 1999, her Harpo Entertainment Group created a new magazine, O, the Oprah Magazine which features Oprah on the cover of every issue. This magazine has become one of the most successful magazines in the country. Naturally, she consistently tops the list of most admired Americans.

Other Black women such as Cathy Hughes are closely behind Oprah. Founding Radio One, Hughes' network consists of 27 stations in 9 major markets with a staff that exceeds 1,500. In 1999 her company went public, with an initial public stock offering that raised $1.2 billion. She maintains 56% control and has grown it to the 16th largest media company in America. Expanding her reach, Hughes now also owns TV One and continues to grow that network.

Ernesta Procope is a lesser known heavyweight. She started her own insurance company in 1952 in Brooklyn. She now has a company that is licensed in all 50 states as the largest minority-owned and female-owned insurance brokerage firm in the country. Her clientele includes some of America's top Fortune 100 companies.

The Black hair-care market was a $1 billion industry in the late 1980s. Realizing the potential, white companies began to compete for business and very quickly half of the market was controlled by white-owned companies.

"Chicago-based Alberto Culver purchased the Dallas-based Pro-Line, founded by Comer Cottrell, the multinational pharmaceutical corporation company. IVAX Corporation purchased Johnson Products, maker of the Ultra-Sheen hair care line in 1993. In 1998, L'Oreal bought Soft Sheen Products that was founded in 1964. Soon L'Oreal owned 50% of the hair-relaxer kit and 62% of hair-coloring markets."[80]

---

80 The Columbia Guide to African American History Since 1939 https://books.google.com/books?id=Y6yuwT54mA0C&pg=PA201&lpg=PA201&dq=history+black+billionaire&source=bl&ots=x00JSlZdnB&sig=lFwaFlR5DvpSY8qrZPVmr4s_q1Q&hl=en&sa=X&ved=0ahUKEwjok6W49YvTAhXIh1QKHcYiD2k4ChDoAQgfMAE#v=onepage&q=history%20black%20billionaire&f=false

While Blacks only comprised 12% of the national population, they controlled 37% of the hair-care market. Only Johnson H. Johnson Fashion Fair Cosmetics remained at the end of the 20th century as a major Black-owned beauty and hair-care products company.

Blacks also thrived in advertising. UniWorld, based in New York, was the largest Black owned advertising agency. In 1999, UniWorld sold 49% of the company to a London-based firm. Around the same time, Burrell Communications Group of Chicago and Essence Communications each sold 49% of their businesses. Essence explained that its sale to AOL-Time Warner would facilitate the company expanding into the Black market to strengthen its presence in beauty and fashion advertising.

Due to most Black leaders selling their companies at some point, much of the historic Black wealth has been lost or not passed down. However, in 2015, the founder of Shea Moisture chose not to sell out and made an historic move. Instead of being taken over by pressures to sell like other recently Black-owned beauty product companies, Richelieu Dennis, by allowing Bain Capital and Target to take a minority stake in his company, maintained superior control and ownership.

In 2017, of the 2,000 billionaires across the world, only 10 of them are Black.

# Oprah Winfrey

Women, Civil and Child Rights Activist, TV Host, Actress, Producer, Author, Philanthropist

Oprah Gail Winfrey was born on January 29, 1954 in Kosciusko, Mississippi in a small farming town. After a tumultuous upbringing, she moved to Nashville with her father. By 1971, she enrolled in Tennessee State University and started working in television broadcasting.

After graduating, Oprah moved to Baltimore, Maryland where she hosted a talk show called People are Talking. She ran that show for eight years until she was recruited by a Chicago TV station to hose her own morning show, AM Chicago. Building from a rough start, she turned the show into a hit by doing it her way. Slowly beating out her competitor, Phil Donahue, she gained 10,000 viewers and exceeded Phil's show for ratings.

Her success led to Steven Spielberg to select her for his 1985 film *The Color Purple*. She also gained an Oscar nomination for Best Supporting Actress. The following year, she launched the *Oprah Winfrey Show* as a nationally syndicated program on 120 channels dispersed across 10 million viewers.

Astonishingly, the show generated $125 million in its first year of production, with Oprah receiving $30 million. Soon after, she gained ownership of her show on ABC and placed it under her own production company, Harpo Productions. This way she made even more money from syndication.

As talk shows grew increasingly trashy with less substance, Oprah vowed to keep her show tabloid free. While losing some interest at first, she eventually bounced back with a resounding, loyal audience.

In 1995, she ran in the Marine Corps Marathon after losing 90 pounds. Her weight loss success helped her chef, Rosie Daley, and trainer, Bob Greene, to release best-selling books.

She literally resurrected the failing book industry by integrating Oprah's book club into her show. This club helped catapult hundreds of little-known authors into immediate, high popularity.

By 1999, she helped co-found Oxygen Media, a cable network for women. This partnership helped her secure her place as one of the most powerful and wealthiest people in the industry. The next year, she released her highly successful magazine, O: The Oprah Magazine.

Adding new life to *The Color Purple*, Oprah helped produce the onstage version for Broadway. The musical, starting Fantastia, received 12 Tony nominations. When the musical was revived by Oprah in 2015, it won the Tony Award for best revival of a musical.

Oprah decided to walk away from her show in 2011 to start OWN, Oprah Winfrey Network in partnership with Discovery Communications.

Overcoming a rough beginning to be properly placed in cable packages, menus and advertisement, the channel made news when Oprah interviewed Lance Armstrong. It was during this famous interview that he confessed to using performance-enhancement drugs.

In a truly boss move, Oprah decided to consolidate Harpo Studios under the Los Angeles-based OWN headquarters. On her OWN network, Oprah returned to acting in Greenleaf, gaining her first recurring role.

Over the decades, Oprah has been increasingly charitable. "Business Week named her the greatest Black philanthropist in American history."[81] Her charity organization, Oprah's Angel Network, has raised more than $51,000,000 for programs including building a school in South Africa for girls, helping with Hurricane Katrina and giving DC public schools $1,000,000.

One of Oprah's major moves for economic development includes her partnership with Habitat for Humanity which has 10,000 volunteers, helping to build houses for impoverished Americans throughout the country. She has also helped countless minority students gain education through her support of A Better Chance, a Boston-based program that provides inner-city youth with the opportunity to attend college preparatory schools.

Life magazine recognizes Oprah Winfrey as the most influential woman of her generation. In 1994, a bill she proposed to President Clinton on child rights was signed into law and directly led to the creation of a nationwide database for child abusers.

She became the first recipient of the Bob Hope Humanitarian Award from the Academy of Television Arts and Sciences in 2002.

Stepping into the political spotlight, Oprah experienced her first-time campaigning for a political candidate as a primary champion for the first Black President, Barack Obama's presidency. Her support attracted donors and large crowds of supporters at rallies. At one event at the University of South Carolina, Oprah attracted nearly 30,000 fans; in an 18,000-seat arena.

In 2013, Oprah Winfrey received the Presidential Medal of Freedom from President Obama and in 2017 CBS announced that will join 60 Minutes as a special contributor, starting in the fall.

Oprah has been in a long-term relationship with Stedman Graham since the 1980s and continues to enjoy her homes with him in Chicago, California, Indiana and Colorado.

---

81  Oprah Winfrey http://www.biography.com/people/oprah-winfrey-9534419

# DeShauna Moore Spencer
Founder, Kweli TV

*Distributing online Black entertainment*

DeShauna Spencer is the Founder/CEO of KweliTV and radio host of emPower Hour on DC's 89.3 FM WPFW. Previously, she served as founding publisher of emPowermagazine.com where she launched the emPower Players Awards honoring community activists of color.

Before becoming an entrepreneur, Spencer served as Director of Communications & Managing Editor for EdMarket. A Memphis native, Spencer graduated from Jackson State University where she studied communications and journalism. She has written for The Clarion-Ledger, The Oakland Tribune, the Crisis Magazine, AOL and the Washington Examiner.

A former AmeriCorps*VISTA and Chips Quinn Scholar, Spencer received a 2012 40under40 award from The Envest Foundation. In 2014, Spencer was honored with the "Who's Got Next" award by the National Action Network. In 2015, Spencer completed her first documentary, Mom Interrupted. She is a Spring 2017 Halcyon Incubator Fellow and a 2017 Voqal Fellow.

# The Great Recession (2008)

*Half of the collective Black wealth was stripped
away during the Great Recession*

THE GREAT RECESSION, spawned by the housing crisis and falling stock markets, was universally hard on America – but none were affected more than the Black community. Even as economic recovery has begun, the wealth gap continues to widen. According to Pew Research Center analysis of data from the Federal Reserve Survey of Consumer Finances, white net worth was 13x higher than Blacks in 2013.[82]

The recession destroyed the net worth of all families, except for those at the top. Unprecedented wealth destruction coupled with high unemployment provided the perfect storm to demonstrate how essential emergency savings are to the long-term financial safety of a family.

There are numerous factors contributing to the widening of the wealth gaps. Median income for Black households dropped 9% since 2010. Thus, minority households have not had a chance to replenish their savings as much as whites. Given that they are also more likely to experience financial emergencies and pay higher fees, it becomes even harder to gain footing on an equal playing field.

---

82  Racial Wealth Gaps. Pew Research. 2014.
http://www.pewresearch.org/fact-tank/2014/12/12/racial-wealth-gaps-great-recession/

Additionally, financial assets such as stocks recovered much faster than housing. Whites are much more likely to own stocks directly than minorities, making them better positioned during the recovery.

The racial gap in the home ownership rate was practically the same in 2000 as it was in 1990 - 25%. As whites increased their home ownership rates, Blacks moved to inner cities where their rates remained low. Black home ownership rates inclined during 1960 – 1980 when the gap was at its smallest, but even then, it was substantial.

The return on home investments is far higher in white families than Blacks. Home equity tends to rise higher for whites than in Black homes. Historic segregation helped to lower demand for Black homes, placing a ceiling on home equity for Black home owners in urban communities.

Whites tend to be more likely to receive and provide inheritances to assist their next generation in homeownership. At the very least, they are more likely to assist with a down payment for their friends and family. With family assistance, larger down payments are usually made by white homebuyers rendering lower interest rates and closing costs. Access to credit and credit scores also play a strong role. Thus, white families began buying homes eight years before Black families on average.

Homeownership is usually the largest investment for any American family. More than half of Black wealth (53%) comes from their home, compared with 39% for whites. The homeownership rate for white families is 28% higher than for Black families.

Since historic discrimination and capital access prevented Blacks from owning homes, the Black community are more recent homeowners, more likely to have high-interest mortgages, more likely to be headed by a single-mother, and more likely to not pass it down to their children. Obviously, Blacks are far more susceptible to foreclosure.

Half of the collective Black wealth was stripped away during the Great Recession; resulting from the lack of equity and high prevalence of predatory loans. Worse, Latinos lost 67% of their total wealth.

Since 2007, 11 million homes have been foreclosed. After adjusting for income and credit scores, it remains a fact that Blacks were unfairly and disproportionately given bad loans. These foreclosures not only impact the immediate families that live in them, but bring down the entire neighborhood. This mere point led to $2 trillion in lost property across the country, half of which is attributed to minorities.

Income impacts whites much differently than Blacks. For every dollar made in the white community it increases by another $5.19 and there is no significant impact on their years of homeownership. In the Black community, that dollar barely doubles at .69 cents and their home is the most important factor in their portfolio. This is largely due to Blacks dominating fields that are less likely to have 401k plans and other benefits. Experiencing more emergencies, Blacks tend to keep the cash they need on stand-by as opposed to whites who tend to invest their disposable income, already having emergency savings.

It goes without saying that white families on average begin with significantly more money and higher incomes than the average Black family. When Blacks and whites start on an equal playing field, their returns mirror each other. In these scenarios, Black families see a growth of $4.03 for each dollar of income.

While most Americans no longer inherit money, whites are five times more likely to inherit money than Blacks and for the amount to be 10 times as what Blacks receive. "Inheritances converted to wealth more readily for white than Black families: each inherited dollar contributed to .91 cents of wealth compared with .20 cents for Black families."[83]

College education is critical to economic success and wealth building. Education is supposed to be the great equalizer but it's not. Family wealth is the largest indicator of educational success. Without this factor, success primarily is depended on the quality of K12 education.

Obviously, with historic segregation, Blacks tend to be isolated in lower-quality schools. For instance, the District of Columbia once boosted a rate of 90% Black students. During this time, DC schools were ranked #51 out of 51.

Cost for higher education has risen by 60% over the last 20 years with the average student loan debt toppling $35,000. 80% of Black students graduate with debt compared with 64 percent of white students. For these reasons,

---

83 Racial Wealth Gap Research Study https://iasp.brandeis.edu/pdfs/Author/shapiro-thomas-m/racialwealthgapbrief.pdf

whites are much more likely to graduate than their undergraduate counterparts. Blacks more often than whites, are forced to leave school to earn an income that will support them and their families.

Over the past 30 years, the gap between students who earn bachelors from low-high income families grew from 31% to 45%. Affluent families spent 5x as much on college for their children as low-income families in 1972 – by 2007 that figure grew to 9x.

Marriage also plays a small role in widening the racial wealth gap. Interestingly, marriage helps to increase wealth for white families by $75,000 but has no significant impact on Blacks. White marriages seem to combine medium wealth profiles to push whites past emergency level savings and into investments.

Black marriages tend to combine much smaller levels of wealth and sometimes just debt, thus having no impact on the new total family wealth.

# Congresswoman Maxine Waters
Civil Rights Activist

Maxine Waters was born on August 15, 1938 in Kintoch, Missouri to Velma and Remus Carr. She was one of thirteen children and raised by a single mother. By 1961, Maxine graduated from high school and moved her family to Los Angeles, California.

Her early employment included work at a garment factory, as a teacher and as a telephone operator. However, she had bigger plans and graduated with a degree in sociology from Los Angeles State College in 1970.

Entering her political career, Maxine started working for Councilman David Cunningham and later entered the California State Assembly in 1976. Her primary roles there would set the stage for the rest of her career. She managed the "divestment of state pension funds from any businesses active in South Africa, a country then operating under the policy of apartheid, and helped pass legislation within the guidelines of the divestment campaign's Sullivan Principles."[84]

84  Maxine Waters https://en.wikipedia.org/wiki/Maxine_Waters

# History of the Black Dollar

In 1990, Maxine Waters was elected to the US House of Representatives with nearly 80% of the popular vote for California's 29th congressional district. Since then, she has been consistently re-elected with at least 70% of the vote.

During the LA riots stemming from the Rodney King verdict, Maxine gained national attention "when she helped deliver relief supplies in Watts and demanded the resumption of vital services." She famously described the protest by saying "if you call it a riot it sounds like it was just a bunch of crazy people who went out and did bad things for no reason. I maintain it was somewhat understandable, if not acceptable."[85]

She was famously called into the spotlight when she purposely interrupted a speech by Peter King (R-NY). Her behavior was called unruly by Carrie Meek, the presiding officer. Carrie a Democrat from Florida, also threatened to have the Sergeant at Arms present her with the Mace of the House of the Representatives. As of 2017, this is still the most recent case of the Mace being suggested for punishment.

Maxine was chair of the Congressional Black Caucus from 1997 to 1998. 10 years later, she served as a superdelegate to the 2008 Demo During the 2008 Democratic National Convention and endorsed Senator Hillary Clinton for the party's nomination. However, with Senator Barack Obama gaining steam, she later switched her endorsement.

The following year, after President Obama was inaugurated, Maxine co-sponsored a bill calling for reparations for slavery in partnership with Rep. John Conyers. In 2011, she demanded the release of millions of jobs to fix the economy by calling for a jobs program of a trillion dollars. She stated "we've got to put Americans to work. That's the only way to revitalize the economy. When people work, they earn money, they spend money, and that's what gets the economy up and going."

In 2012, Maxine became the ranking member of the House Financial Services Committee.

On March 27, 2014, she introduced the Housing Opportunities Move the Economy Forward Act, better known as the HOME Forward Act of 2014. This

---

85 Pandey, Swati (April 29, 2007). "Was it a 'riot,' a 'disturbance' or a 'rebellion'?". Los Angeles Times. Retrieved May 12, 2010.

key provision included the "collection of 10 basis points for every dollar out-standing mortgages collateralizing covered securities estimated to be approximately $5 billion a year. These funds would be directed to three funds that support affordable housing initiatives, with 75% going to the National Housing Trust Fund."[86] The priority of the National Housing Trust Fund is to allow states to build, preserve, rehabilitate and operate affordable rental housing to low-income families via state block grants. These funds have a hyper focus on seniors, the disabled and minimum wage workers.

In 2017, she drew even more public attention and further immortalized herself in civil rights history when she publicly stated that she was waiting on Trump's impeachment and listed several reasons he was causing the country "chaos and division."

# Michael Kevin Floyd
Founder, PurchaseAlly (formerly Inspectivize)

*Customizing custom real estate experiences*

For many people, buying a house represents fulfilling a dream. A Baltimore startup wants to make sure home inspections don't add a nightmarish quality to the process.

While working as a home inspector, Michael Floyd found customers had issues with the process of finding the right home inspection company for the right type of inspection (Lead paint or termites? Mold or Radon?) in the right geographical area.

Floyd and a small team are building Inspectivize to make the booking process easier. When considering building such an app for his company, Floyd said he realized, "Why not build a platform that will be available for every inspection company?"

After entering criteria including the type of inspection, date and ZIP code, the app uses an algorithm that offers homeowners and realtors the top three

---

86  Maxine Waters https://en.wikipedia.org/wiki/Maxine_Waters

matches for inspectors. Customers can then review the ratings and other info about the services, and decide which to book.

The web and mobile app is also designed to notify users that inspectors are en route, and process payments. It has room for up to eight scheduled inspections.

In addition to helping homeowners find an inspector, the app can reduce the risk of getting overcharged. Inspection prices often fluctuate since they are not regulated. Introducing a side-by-side comparison can add transparency, Floyd said.

Floyd believes it will also help the inspection companies by providing a place for marketing. Just as the customers have trouble finding what they need, the companies can find it difficult to stand out.

"It's a great business to be in, but the competition is fierce. You have to be able to market, and realtors have to be aware that the company exists," he said. Many currently use Google AdWords, through which companies pay to be listed first.

Inspectivize will help the companies get in front of the very customers who want their services, Floyd said.

Joining Floyd in building the company is cofounder and Morgan State University professor Celeste Chavis. Morgan State engineering and computer science student Joshua Fitchett, who is also a teaching assistant with CodePath, is the company's CTO.

*Extracted from Stephen Babcock, Technically Baltimore*

# The Black Financial Experience (2011)

*"I've been consistent in saying that, you know, this is a legacy of a troubled racial past, of Jim Crow and slavery. That's not an excuse for Black folks, and I think the overall majority of Black people understand it's not an excuse. They're working hard. They're out there hustling and trying to get an education, trying to send their kids to college, but they're starting behind oftentimes in the race."*

— PRESIDENT BARACK OBAMA

TODAY ONLY 5% of Black households have a net worth above $350,000. Less than 1% of Black families have over a million in net assets. The average white family has a net worth of $116,000 dollars. Sadly, when you deduct the family car as an asset, the average Black family in America only has a net worth of $1,700. Even worse, 40% of Blacks have 0 or negative net worth.

These figures are decreasing not rising for Blacks. In 2009, the average white household held wealth of $113,149 compared with $5,677 for Black families.

In 2012, Angel Rich conceived the first African American Financial Experience study at Prudential Financial. It was the first time a financial services company had conducted a primary research study to understand the financial attitudes, perspective and behavior of the Black community. The study contained many groundbreaking results, including the fact that Blacks owned more life insurance than other races at an equal or higher value, learned financial literacy best through churches, was 3x as likely as whites to withdraw from their 401k and 1 in 3 desired to be entrepreneurs. This spawned a conversation about economic inequality and marketing for those that were really trying to figure out how to now sell financial products to the Black community. In fact, New York Life launched a $50 billion, 100-year plan to go after the Black community and Morgan Stanley ordered a copy for every single employee, globally. Other companies like JP Morgan Chase partnered with organizations such as the Center for Global Policy Solutions to discover innovative ways for reducing economic inequality.

Shortly after, Angel Rich founded her company The Wealth Factory and conducted another research study sponsored by the Charter School Development Corporation and Building Hope – The Financial Empowerment of Urban Youth. The study revealed key components that lead to the wealth inequality gap in the Black community and providing real solutions for closing the gap. It was presented and adopted by the Department of Education as well as Department of Insurance, Securities and Banking. Some of the most important discoveries include the impact of gamification on learning financial literacy in underserved communities, especially amongst people with special needs. Rich also highlighted that affluent children spend 1,200 more hours in novel locations (places outside of their neighborhood) gaining exposure to a myriad of things that Blacks are usually not exposed to, emphasizing the need for more field trips and summer enrichment experiences.

One month later, Congresswoman Maxine Waters released her report, building on her long history of economic development in the Black community and bringing the topic to the nation's attention. Her findings mirrored Rich's report and gave further credence to best practices for closing the wealth inequality gap.

Meeting Angel Rich at the release of her report in DC, the Congresswoman then invited her to her office. Rich then met with her team and received the full support of her office to use her name as needed in the movement to close the racial wealth gap.

Since then, several evaluations of Black and white wealth in America have been produced. The National Urban League released the State of Black America, compiling data to create indexes; and Pew Research released data detailing the median net worth of Black families compared to whites.

There are roughly 120 million American households, with 14 million of them being Black. Just 1.4% of the top 1% is Black — 16,800 homes. Their median net asset worth is $1.2 million.

Nearly 10% of white households, totaling over 8 million families have more than 1.3 million in net worth. A recent study by the Federal Reserve Survey of Consumer Finances released shocking (to some) figures that made it "unequivocally clear how small the number of Black families is that have access to wealth required to send children to universities, start businesses or put money down for home loans for their children."

"If you're white and have a net worth of about $356,000 dollars that's good enough to put you in the 72$^{nd}$ percentile of white families. If you're Black, it's good enough to catapult you into the 95$^{th}$ percentile. Only 700,000 of the 14 million Black homes have more than $356,000 dollars in total net worth."

William Darity, Professor of Public Policy, African and African-American Studies and Economics at Duke University told the Duke Chronicle that "the major sources of wealth for most of the super-rich are inheritances and in life transfers. The big reason is racial differences in access to resources to transfer to the next generation." He went on to say that "the practices of enslavement violence, Jim Crow, discrimination and dispossession of property have kept generations of African Americans from accruing the type of wealth that whites in the top 1 percent have today."[87]

According to Matt Bruenig of Demos.org, "white families hold 90 percent of the national wealth. Hispanic families hold 2.3 percent and Blacks hold 2.6 percent of the national wealth." While there may be the 'Decadent Veil', where a small group of wealthy Black celebrities and athletes are highlighted in in media, it could not be further from the truth for the race as a whole[88].

It is also clear that access to opportunity by color has had a lasting effect on history and continues to dictate the future. Thomas Shapiro, author of The Roots of the Widening Racial Wealth Gap, followed the same households for 25 years, finding that their total wealth gap nearly tripled — increasing from

---

87 5% of African American Households Have More Than $350,000 in net worth http://www.eurweb.com/2015/11/only-5-of-african-american-households-have-more-than-350000-in-net-worth/#

88 America's Financial Divide http://www.huffingtonpost.com/antonio-moore/americas-financial-divide_b_7013330.html

$85,000 in 1984 to $236,500 in 2009. He feels the biggest drivers of the growing wealth gap is years of homeownership, household income, unemployment, higher education, inheritance, family support and pre-existing family wealth. The number of years of homeownership is the largest predictor of the wealth gap growth by race.

Most fascinating, Shapiro was not able to find a common thread of "what underlies the ability to build wealth, including the notion that personal attributes and behavioral choices are key pieces of the equation. Instead, the evidence points to policy and the configuration of both opportunities and barriers in workplaces, schools, and communities that reinforce deeply entrenched racial dynamics in how wealth is accumulated and that continue to permeate the most important spheres of everyday life." Data for this derived from the Panel Study of Income Dynamics, a nationally representative longitudinal study that began in 1968. "The compelling evidence-based story is that policy shaping opportunities and rewards where we live, where we learn, and where we work propels the large majority of the widening racial wealth gap.

"The general policy direction of trying to increase demand for Black labor in local economies is sound. But much more policy experimentation and research needs to be done to determine how best to improve the local economic climate facing Blacks" as stated by T. J. Bartik of the Upjohn Institute in his technical report, Economic Development and Black Economic Success.

# Aaron Saunders

Founder, Inclusive Innovation Incubator and Clearly Innovative

*Equaling the playing field for Black founders*

Aaron Saunders is the CEO and Founder of Clearly Innovative Inc., a minority-owned digital solutions provider headquartered in Washington DC. The firm shapes ideas into viable products and transforms clients' existing technologies into stunning digital solutions. Clearly Innovative is a leader in early adaption and implementation of cutting edge technologies to create web and mobile solutions, exemplifying this through work for the National Museum of African American History and Culture, Queens Public Library, and even the American Red Cross, to name a few. Clearly Innovative provides support and expertise through services focused on product strategy, user experience, design and development.

Aaron, through his company Cleary Innovative, has demonstrated commitment to preparing future generations for the Innovation Economy. In 2012, Clearly Innovative provided STEM and entrepreneurship classes, piloting a Summer program at Howard University Middle School for Math and Science (HUMS).

Demonstrating success at HUMS through two consecutive first place wins, for our students, in the Verizon App Challenge, the education initiative began to expand. After being awarded a $100,000 grant from Chase Bank's Mission Main Street to focus on extending the work of the education initiatives, Clearly Innovative branded its education work Luma Lab, Inc. Through a partnership with TDF Foundation, Luma Lab provides free and subsidized STEM based after-school and summer programs at DC Public schools and the Boys & Girls Club of Greater Washington. Aaron and his company have been recognized for their mobile development and education work being covered on NBC news, NPR, Washington Business Journal, and more. Aaron himself was recognized as MMTC's Champion of Digital Equality at their annual Access to Capital and Telecom Policy Summit and was one of nine entrepreneurs selected to be featured on the Washington Business Journal's 2017 Book of Lists.

To further validate the education initiatives, since Luma Lab's inception nearly 1,000 students and adults in the District of Columbia have been provided with unique opportunities and exposure to technology and business education. Partnerships have grown to include the College Success Foundation, AnBryce Foundation, Georgetown Day School, KIPP Will Academy, YWCA, and the Development Corp. of Columbia Heights.

Most recently Clearly Innovative was selected by Howard University and DC Mayor Muriel Bowser to operate the Inclusive Innovation Incubator (In3) at Howard University. Currently set to open on April 17, 2017, In3 will be the District's first incubator, training, and co-working facility intentionally focused on increasing diversity in tech and business. The incubator will offer entrepreneurship training, co-working space, events space, mentorship and a cross sector experience that bridges the gap between DC's multifaceted education, business and tech industries.

Aaron's passion for education is also showcased through his work as an Adjunct Computer Science Professor at Howard University teaching courses on Web and Mobile Development. His unique perspective working with clients to quickly create solutions or long-term product strategy creates a relevant and hands-on approach to teaching web and mobile development with a focus on creativity and innovation.

Aaron has over thirty-years of experience in the technology and innovation space he has strong technical, communication, and collaboration abilities. He is highly adept at helping organizations add business value using technology. Aaron is recognized in the space as the thought-leader on mobile development and his book "Building Cross-Platform Apps using Titanium, Alloy, and Appcelerator Cloud Services" was published in November 2014. Aaron has a BS in Computer Science from Ohio Wesleyan University and an MBA in Information Technology Strategy and Marketing from the NYU Stern School of Business.

# Stephanie Lampkin
Founder, Blendoor

*Crafting financial equality through blind job matching*

Stephanie Lampkin learned to code at age 13. By 15, she was a full-stack web developer, fluent in the languages of computer programming. She has a Stanford engineering degree and an MBA from MIT.

Still, she recalls making it to the eighth round of interviews in pursuit of a gig at a well-known tech firm in Silicon Valley, only to be told her background wasn't "technical enough" for a role in software engineering.

"The recruiter told me a sales or marketing job might open up," she said. She ended up at Microsoft MSFT +1.70%, where she spent five years in a technical role. Still, she wonders about that early rejection, and whether being a young African-American woman hurt her chances.

This month, Lampkin is set to launch a job matching tool aimed at removing just that sort of lingering doubt from the tech sector job hunt.

Her app Blendoor lets job seekers upload resumes, then hides their name and photo from employers. The idea, says Lampkin, is to circumvent unconscious bias by removing gender and ethnicity from the equation.

In the course of her research, Lampkin found a National Bureau of Economic Research study showing that a "white-sounding" name (Emily or Greg, for example) can yield as many job callbacks as an additional eight years of experience for someone with an "African-American sounding" name (Lakisha or Jamal, in the experiment).

"It's quantifiable," Lampkin said. "We realized that hiding names and photos created a safer space. Women and people of color felt better sharing their information."

Blendoor will go live on March 11th at this year's SXSW digital festival for public beta testing. So far, Lampkin has had buy-in from 19 large tech firms. She aims to have 50 on the app in the near future.

She didn't approach any companies that don't already have strong diversity initiatives in place. Intel INTC +1.25%, with its $300 million commitment to diversity, was a natural fit. So was Google GOOGL +2.38%, which devoted $150 million to expanding its talent pool in 2015 alone. Facebook FB +1.24% and Apple are also on board.

"My company resonates more with white men when I position it as, 'hey, I want to help you find the best talent. Your unconscious mind isn't racist, sexist -- it's totally natural, and we're trying to help you circumvent it.'"

Lampkin hopes women, people of color, members of the LGBT community and other minorities in Silicon Valley who may feel alienated by job search tools that prominently display one's name and headshot will feel comfortable using Blendoor.

"I know a number of really successful, Ivy League-educated, African-American people between about 35 and 45 who refuse to use LinkedIn out of fear of discrimination," she said.

"These [online networking] companies are founded by white guys. There's a psychology I understand as a woman of color that's driven how and why I've shaped the product the way I have."

The app will, of course, be collecting useful stats on who exactly is applying to tech's most sought-after positions and who is getting "matched", in the app's parlance, with jobs. "Blendoor wants to make companies accountable using data," Lampkin said.

If all goes according to plan, she may well test Blendoor's technology in the venture capital world, where minorities -- black women, especially -- have made little headway, either as investors or recipients of VC backing.

"When you think about it, names and photos are not necessary for the transaction," said Lampkin.

She herself has raised $100,000 in pre-seed funding for Blendoor. Half of that came from Pipeline Angels, a network of women investors and social entrepreneurs funding diverse companies. More than 20% of the businesses funded to date have a black woman at the helm.

*Extracted from Clare O'Connor, Forbes*

# Black Lives Matter (2012)

*#HandsUpDontShoot*

#BLACKLIVESMATTER WAS BORN in 2012 after Trayvon Martin's murderer, George Zimmerman, was acquitted for his crime – killing unarmed 17-year old Trayvon while wearing a hoodie and carrying an Arizona ice tea.

While the phrase entered, the social scene following Zimmerman's acquittal, it didn't take shape until 2014, when Ferguson police officer Darren Wilson killed Michael Brown. The hashtag would sometimes receive more than 100,000 tweets per day.

As its usage rose, other hashtags associated with police complaints died such as #HandsUpDontShoot and #NoJusticeNoPeace. This helped to grow the movement with #BlackLivesMatter as the common theme in social justice situations.

The three mothers who coined the term co-founded the Black Lives Matter network, which has dozens of chapters in the major urban cities. They quickly mobilized their power into a grassroots organization for large protests and testimonies, leveraging their political power[89].

Black Lives Matter is a chapter-based national organization working for the validity of Black life; working to rebuild the Black liberation movement.[90]

---

89 The Dynamic history of #BlackLivesMatter Explained http://www.huffingtonpost.com/entry/history-black-lives-matter_us_56d0a3b0e4b0871f60eb4af5

90 http://blacklivesmatter.com/about/

A consortium of more than 50 civil rights groups came together in 2016 as the Movement for Black Lives with an agenda for reparations, investing in Black communities and economic justice. "The issues dealing with race and racism and racial inequality in the United States are intimately connected to the issues of wealth inequality" said Patrick Mason, Chair of the National Economic and Social Rights Initiative. Mason argues that the tax code, especially estate tax and capital gains tax, is one of the primary contributors to wealth inequality. Black Lives Matter call for an increase on both of those taxes and would like to end income caps on payroll taxes that fund Social Security and unemployment.[91]

Momentum for economic justice has been growing since the high-profile killings of unarmed Black men at the hands of police, many who were low income. Following the death of Michael Brown in Ferguson, Missouri, the Justice Department investigation determined that the police had excessively stopped Blacks, often giving them multiple tickets in one stop.

According to Dedrick Asante-Muhammad, Director of the Racial Wealth Divide Initiative at the Corporation for Enterprise Development, the issues that Black Lives Matter protest are directly linked to the economy.

Black Lives Matter is requesting money that is usually earmarked for prisons to be redirected to education, employment and other human care services in Black communities. They are calling for an end to money bail, incarceration fees, and criminal history checks for housing, loans and employment. They feel reparations are due for the wealth lost from slavery, racism, and other institutional discrimination.

# Economic Justice Proposal

Black Lives Matter demands economic justice for all and a reconstruction of the economy to ensure Black communities have collective ownership, not merely access. This includes

1. A progressing restructuring of tax codes at the local, state, and federal levels to ensure a radical and sustainable redistribution of wealth.

---

91 Black Lives Matter activists are expanding their call for justice to new a target: the economy http://money.cnn.com/2016/08/02/news/economy/black-lives-matter-the-economy/

2. Federal and state job programs that specifically target the most economically marginalized Black people, and compensation for those involved in the care economy. Job programs must provide a living wage and encourage support for local workers' centers, unions, and Black-owned businesses which are accountable to the community.

3. A right to restored land, clear air, clean water and housing and an end to the exploitative privatization of natural resources – including land and water. We seek democratic control over how resources are preserved, used and distributed and do so while honoring and respecting the rights of our Indigenous family.

4. The right for workers to organize in public and private sectors especially in "On Demand Economy" jobs.

5. Restore the Glass-Steagall Act to break up the large banks, and call for the National Credit Union Administration and the US Department of the Treasury to change policies and practices around regulation, reporting and consolidation to allow for the continuation and creation of Black banks, small and community development credit unions, insurance companies and other financial institutions.

6. An end to the Trans-Pacific Partnership and a renegotiation of all trade agreements to prioritize the interest of workers and communities.

7. Through tax incentives, loans and other government directed resources, support the development of cooperative or social economy networks to help facilitate trade across and in Black communities globally. All aid in the form of grants, loans, or contracts to help facilitate this must go to Black led or Black supported networks and organizations as defined by the communities.

8. Financial support of Black alternative institutions including policy that subsidizes and offers low-interest, interest-free or federally guaranteed low-interest loans to promote the development of cooperatives, land trusts and culturally responsive health infrastructures that serve the collective needs of our communities.

9. Protection for workers in industries that are not appropriately regulated including domestic workers, farm workers, and tipped workers, and

for workers — many of whom are Black women and incarcerated people — who have been exploited and remain unprotected. This includes the immediate passage at the Federal and state level of the Domestic Workers Bill of Rights and extension of worker protections to incarcerated people.

# Congressman Elijah Cummings
Civil Rights Advocate

Elijah Cummings was born the son of a South Carolina sharecropper on January 18, 1951 to Ruth and Robert Cummings. He was one of seven children.

By 1969, he graduated with honors from Baltimore City College. He later graduated from Howard University with a Bachelor of Arts in Political Science in 1973. He became a noted member of Phi Beta Kappa while at Howard.

In 1976, he graduated from law school at the University of Maryland and was admitted to the Maryland Bar in 1976. Elijah practiced law for 19 years before being elected in 1996.

Interestingly, he has received 12 honorary doctoral degrees from different universities across America. He has a large part of time levering his position to improve health care and education in urban communities.

He started representing a Black district in West Baltimore in the Maryland Hose of Delegates in 1983, serving for 14 years. As a member of the Maryland General Assembly, he was Chairman of the Legislative Black Caucus of Maryland.

Elijah addressed the Democratic National Convention on racial equality in 2016 saying "Our party does not just believe, but understands, that Black Lives Matter. But we also recognize that our community and our law enforcement work best when they work together."[92]

---

92 Cummings declare Black Lives Matter in convention speech http://www.politico.com/story/2016/07/elijah-cummings-black-lives-matter-226157

He serves on many boards including the United States Naval Academy Board of Visitors and Baltimore Zoo Board of Trustees. He is an active member of the New Psalmist Baptist Church and married to Dr. Maya Rockeymoore.

# Victor "Divine" Lombard
Founder, The Black Card

*Rapping for rights to creating tech for banking*

Divine is a Hip-Hop/Rap recording artist and Rapper heavily entrenched in Hip-Hop culture and has been rapping since a very young age. His raps are comprised of deft lyricism with an intelligent, philosophical, social and political world view, spirituality and real life street themes he weaves into intoxicating urban poetry. He now brings this sophisticated rap style and thought process to tech, merging the worlds of Hip-Hop and technology seamlessly in his rhymes. So much so, that he created a new sub-genre within Hip-Hop and Rap that he calls "Tech-Hop".

Divine is a disruptor in every sense of the word with his relentless ambition, determination, grind and hustle. He first appeared on the tech community radar in 2014 when he reached out to famed tech venture capitalist Ben Horowitz, Co-Founder of top-tier Silicon Valley tech VC firm Andreessen Horowitz (a16z) on social media via Twitter and the two eventually became friends. Ben, who is an avid Hip-Hop and Rap fan himself can readily be found hanging out with such Hip-Hop and Rap heavyweights such as Nas and Kanye West among others. Ben and his wife Felicia Horowitz would then pledge to Divine's Kickstarter project for Divine's debut album "Ghetto Rhymin'". Divine's tribute song and video to Ben, "Venture Capitalist (Like Ben Horowitz)" would follow, along with numerous articles written about their "unlikely friendship" appearing on such tech websites as TechCrunch SF, Tech Cocktail and Valleywag.

The Valleywag article would become controversial for its sarcastic, undermining, disparaging and racist undertones relative to the friendship and Ben's preference in the company he keeps as well as the music he loves. So much so that Divine would then write an open letter to the author of the article eloquently reprimanding her for writing such a negative article with no real substance beyond simply criticizing the friendship, Ben and attempts at undermining them both. This would lead to a 24-hour Twitter campaign storm from the tech community supporting Divine, Ben and their friendship. Ben himself would even join in and tweet in defense of Divine, strongly addressing and reprimanding both the author and Valley Wag's Editor who had a history of writing sarcastic, critical and undermining articles criticizing and attacking Ben. However, this controversy would immediately spill over into a positive article being written on Ben for Forbes, with Divine's story linked within it.

Divine and Ben would meet for the first time in person when Hip-Hop and tech organization The Phat Startup's Co-Founder James Lopez invited Divine to their event Startups Are Hard: Keeping It Real with Ben Horowitz in NYC. Divine, who is a former substantial drug dealer and felon who only completed the 8th grade and is self-taught with over 10 years of incarceration in federal prison and with no tech background, credits Ben for inspiring and motivating him to pursue entrepreneurship specifically in technology determined to change his life around. This determination would lead Divine to enrolling in Defy Ventures, an entrepreneurship program for ex-offenders with the challenge of "transforming your hustle", which would find him at Harvard Business School (HBS) being taught by five renowned HBS professors for a day.

Divine would go on to write a theme rap song intro for the a16z podcast where he predicted the merge of Facebook and virtual reality (VR) company Oculus prior to the official deal happening. That theme rap song led Ben to call Divine the "official a16z rapper". He was also officially given the honor to be the first (and currently only) person to narrate blog posts from Ben's popular blog Ben's Blog which is read by nearly 10 million people worldwide. He would continue to narrate other posts from Ben's partner and Co-Founder of a16z, Marc Andreessen, as well as famed VC Mark Suster of Upfront Ventures and Techstars.

In late 2014, these developments would connect Divine with tech entrepreneur Shaherose Charania, CEO and Founder of Women 2.0 that produces the Women 2.0 Conference. Shaherose invited Divine to be a part of the conference where he was briefly interviewed by Shaherose and performed in front of a room filled with mostly women in tech. Divine performed "Venture Capitalist (Like Ben Horowitz)", as well as debuted and performed another Tech-Hop song, "VC Life (By Any Means)", a second song he created to further convey his burgeoning relationship with Ben.

These events would compel celebrity street wear entrepreneur and visionary Greg Selkoe, Founder and CEO at the time of Boston based Karmaloop to reach out to Divine and build a business relationship that would ultimately lead to him being hired by Selkoe as a paid intern to the CEO and Entrepreneur In Residence at Karmaloop in January of 2015.

Continually strengthening his presence and network throughout Silicon Valley, Divine would have the ultimate honor of connecting with and being coached by leadership strategist, advisor, innovation coach and tech veteran Ellen P. Leanse, Founder of Karmahacks and formerly of Apple, Google and Facebook who was named one of Tech's Top 5 Marketers and named a Silicon Valley Woman of Influence.

Also in 2015, Divine was tapped by tech VC Karl Mehta of Silicon Valley tech VC firm Menlo Ventures and CEO and Founder of EdCast, to create a Tech-Hop song for his new startup EdCast, a knowledge network and social learning platform. Divine created and then performed the song, "EdCasting", at Stanford University in front of a room full of academics and other notable individuals in edtech. Divine took the stage after the former U.S. Secretary of Defense Dr. William Perry and after his performance was hailed by Microsoft's SR Business Program Manager Rhonda Nicholson who excitedly suggested to Karl, "Let's post the rapper song front and center on the [EdCast] portal - loved it!"

This same year Divine made his speaking debut at the Hip-Hop and tech conference Tech808 Oakland under the billing: "Building with Divine – From Crack to Rap to Tech", which is produced by The Phat Startup, to an overwhelmingly positive response with a following Tech Crunch write-up. With Divine's unique infectious and magnetic and inspiring and motivational energy, he confidently relayed his redemptive life journey from a substantial crack dealer and lengthy federal incarceration to his entrance into tech via Ben, he even did a surprise performance of "VC Life (By Any Means)". Divine then returned later this year to Tech808 NYC to perform as well as debut the fully illustrated and animated video "VC Life (By Any Means)".

Divine was then tapped by Kingonomics creator and author Rodney Sampson, a veteran tech investor, to be a part of the Kingonomics: Westside Edition event where Divine spoke at five Atlanta Public Schools in three days telling his story "From Crack To Rap To Tech" inspiring and motivating students to higher education and career paths emphasizing entrepreneurship and technology. That event culminated in a Q&A with Divine and a Tech-Hop performance. Mr. Sampson would note that amongst all the guests, Divine's presence and story resonated most with the high school students and left a strong positive impression on them.

Divine would then be given the honor and invited by HypeFresh Magazine CEO & Co-Founder Clark Kennedy to do a Q&A, speak and share his story at Philadelphia's Temple University with students in a Black Media class conducted by Professor Timothy N. Welbeck, Esq. in the Department of African American Studies.

Divine was also featured as a guest on The Karen Hunter Show's "Tech Tuesday" in December 2015 where he was interviewed by Ms. Hunter concerning his early childhood as a crack dealer, his entrance into tech and his BLAK Card fintech product. Karen Hunter is a Pulitzer Prize-Winning Journalist, Publisher, Professor, Bestselling Author and Host. The Karen Hunter Show broadcasts live from NYC on SiriusXM Urban View (Channel 126).

Only over a year and a half after meeting Ben, Divine had his own independent three-part Q&A article with Will Hayes, CEO of Lucidworks for Forbes concerning his story, Hip-Hop and Silicon Valley and diversity and inclusion in tech published and is now a professional Motivational Inspirer, via his own 4th Letter Media company, utilizing his extraordinary life story and journey to motivate and inspire others and assist in solving the problem of diversity and inclusion in tech.

In early 2015 Divine would found a fintech startup, BLAK FINTECH, a financial services and technology company that builds affordable technology driven personal financial and banking products with a focus on the financially excluded. BLAK's first product is the BLAK Card, a next generation prepaid debit card attached to a real bank account powered by banking system technology, integrating a social impact component consisting of financial literacy and entrepreneurship education for wealth building.

Subsequently, 2016 would have BLAK Fintech being accepted into the Village Capital FinTech US 2016 program in partnership with PayPal. (Divine would go on to complete the program in September 2016.)

Around this same time Divine was also tapped by San Francisco music technology company Rhymeo to be an advisor and brand ambassador to assist Rhymeo in authentically marketing to an urban Hip-Hop/Rap audience. Rhymeo is a freestyle rap app and is the only app that gives visual and linguistic material to help you rap.

He is currently working on his first book, "Tweet Out Into The Ether: From Crack To Rap To Tech", a title he says was borrowed from Felicia from a speech she had given about his life at GLIDE Memorial Church in San Francisco. The book will also contain a foreword written by Ben. Additionally, a screenplay is in the works to make a film on Divine's life and journey that will include a soundtrack of original music by Divine and other urban music recording artists.

Although new to the technology world Divine has embraced it and has ambitious plans of entrepreneurial pursuits in the industry with the ultimate goal of becoming a venture capitalist, like Ben Horowitz.

# Closing the Racial Wealth Gap (2017)

*Financial empowerment is essential to the
future of the Black Community.*

— *Angel Rich*

THE ECONOMIC CONTENT of the Black community is seemingly missing from the pages of Black history. The racial wealth gap not only hurts Black families, it limits the nation's economic growth and innovation. In America, the richest 1% of households own 37% of all wealth. This rancid inequality has deep-seated historical roots and continues to be exasperated by current political decision makers that indulge the affluent.

The point of studying the lives and businesses of these heroes is to demonstrate the connection Blacks have always maintained with entrepreneurship and capitalism. This review is not just a reflection of wealth that was acquired, but also land accumulation, innovation and influence. A focus on income and wealth and the fine lines of difference in between is important.

The financial goals of Blacks strongly correlate with a focus on their family's health and future. Core issues of concern include education, leaving money behind and helping the community. Compared to other populations, making charitable donations is a higher priority for Blacks (68% v. 55%).[93]

---

93 The African American Financial Experience Study 2012 prudential.com/africanamericans

The award-winning CNN investigative series, Black in America, found that one of out of every three Black families are at risk of falling out of middle class status due to unemployment, overspending and unexpected financial crises.[94]

Financial capability is the capacity, based on knowledge, skills, and access, to manage financial resources effectively[95]. Youth are most susceptible to financial vulnerability, obstacles to financial growth, and lack of resources. Building skills through education and environmental explorations is the most important key to growing the financial future of Black youth.

Throughout history, some Blacks were blatant and unmasked in their expression of hatred towards race inequality like Nat Turner and others were subtle with their approach like Booker T. Washington. Neither approach is better than the other. Both styles are necessary to build a cohesive picture and enforce a specific future of equality.

"In reviewing Black political economy and alternative economic traditions, Gordon Nembhard makes it clear how much economic thinking has receded in the past several decades. Instead of Black manifestos, calls for reparations, and Black owned cooperatives, contemporary writing concentrates more narrowly on individual accomplishments than on the ways that market failures… the concept of economic resistance is rarely examined.[96]"

On January 1, 1863, the Emancipation Proclamation declared that all slaves were now free.

Starting in 1961, Martin Luther King repeatedly asked John F. Kennedy for a second Emancipation Proclamation to end segregation. A 1961 telegram to Kennedy requested a "second Emancipation Proclamation to free all Negroes from second class citizenship" in concert with the "defense of democratic principles and practices" in the US.[97]

---

94  http://www.npr.org/templates/story/story.php?storyId=130589817

95  Department of the Treasury, *Amended Charter: President's Advisory Council on Financial Capability.* http://www.treasury.gov/resource-center/financialeducation/ Documents/PACFC%202010%20Amended%20Charter.pdf.

96  Why is Economic Content Missing from African American History https://www.jstor.org/ stable/40034436?seq=5#page_scan_tab_contents

97  http://kingencyclopedia.stanford.edu/encyclopedia/encyclopedia/enc_emancipation_ proclamation_1893/

# History of the Black Dollar

During the 1963 March on Washington, King noted that the Emancipation Proclamation provided hope to Black slaves. The following year, Congress passed the Civil Rights Act of 1964.[98] While the Civil Rights Act may have won the battle against segregation, it did not win the war of emancipating all Negroes from second class citizenship.

There is a top-down and bottom-up approach that needs to be applied to close the racial wealth gap. Public policies play an essential role from the top-down in creating equal opportunity for employment, housing, education, small business and retirement plans.

It must be of the utmost priority to have fair lending practices and fair housing policies enforced across the country. The goal of this effort should be to deteriorate traces of residential segregation, build diverse communities that support diverse people and form a legacy of generational wealth through homeownership.

Stable and increasing incomes is the primary resource for wealth accumulation. The minimum wage should be raised and tools such as Blendoor, by Stephanie Lampkin, that decrease demographical biases in hiring practices should be used to enforce equal pay for equal work and credentials. Games such as CreditStacker, by Angel Rich, should be used to engage families in financial literacy, teach credit management, avoid debt and become financially savvy.

Affordable, high-quality childhood development is critical to increasing wealth amongst the masses. Black children are being lost "in the cycle" before they even finish elementary school. Prisons are being constructed based on the reading levels of Black boys in the 3rd grade.

The National Society of Black Engineers discovered that the math score of the average Black student is a direct indication of their future wealth.

Policies that end the school-prison pipeline and more strongly hold the values of ensuring all youth attend college need to be more prevalent. But most importantly, universities must stop raising tuition rates, strapping students from all backgrounds with huge amounts of debt.

Inheritance must be taken much more seriously in the Black community.

---

98 http://kingencyclopedia.stanford.edu/encyclopedia/encyclopedia/enc_emancipation_proclamation_1893/

Much of our original wealth originated from life insurance so we must return to the philosophy of leaving funds to the next generation. Otherwise, each generation will continue to start from a pit that takes nearly half a lifetime to escape from and gain footing on an even level playing field[99].

When comparing the racial wealth gap between Blacks and whites, researchers note that at the current rate it will take more than 200 years for Blacks to become economically equal to whites. Action is needed now.

# Keys to Closing the Racial Wealth Gap

1.  Equal family wealth
2.  Equal income for same level of work
3.  Emergency savings stored
4.  Long-term home ownership
5.  Reduced barriers for unemployment and growth
6.  Access to capital, credit and benefits
7.  Restructuring community development

## Dr. Maya Rockeymoore
President and CEO, Center for Global Policy Solutions

Dr. Maya Rockeymoore is President and CEO of Global Policy Solutions, a Washington, D.C. based consulting firm and President of the Center for Global Policy Solutions, a 501c3 nonprofit organization dedicated to making policy work for people and their environments. Dr. Rockeymoore has previously served as the Vice President of Research and Programs at the Congressional Black Caucus Foundation (CBCF), Senior Resident Scholar for Health and Income Security at the National Urban League, Chief of Staff to Congressman Charles Rangel (D-NY), Professional Staff on the House Ways and Means Committee, and as

---

99  Roots of the Widening Racial Wealth Gap
https://iasp.brandeis.edu/pdfs/Author/shapiro-thomas-m/racialwealthgapbrief.pdf

a CBCF Legislative Fellow in the office of Congressman Melvin Watt (D-NC) among other positions.

Dr. Rockeymoore has presented and written extensively about health disparities, childhood obesity, health care reform, community-based approaches to health, HIV/AIDS, and Medicaid and Medicare policy. She is the co-author of the Action Strategies for Healthy Communities Toolkit and she has published articles in the American Journal of Preventive Medicine and the National Association of State Boards of Education's State Education Standard among other publications. A member of the National Academy of Social Insurance, Dr. Rockeymoore contributed to the development of its seminal study panel report, "Strengthening Medicare's Role in Reducing Racial and Ethnic Health Disparities."

Dr. Rockeymoore is also a widely sought after economic security expert. She has spoken extensively on jobs and the economy, the racial wealth gap, financial literacy, and Social Security. She is the co-editor of Strengthening Community: Social Insurance in a Diverse America and the co-author of Plan for a New Future: The Impact of Social Security Reform on Communities of Color. Dr. Rockeymoore has been invited to testify before Congress on income security matters and on February 23, 2009 she was among other nationally renowned economic and income security experts selected to attend the Obama Administration's White House Fiscal Responsibility Summit.

Dr. Rockeymoore has extensive education policy and program experience. In addition to working on education policy while serving as Chief of Staff to Congressman Charles Rangel in the U.S. House of Representatives, Dr. Rockeymoore has worked with some of the nation's leading progressive education advocacy organizations to advance an agenda focused on strengthening public education for vulnerable children. From 2005-2007, Dr. Rockeymoore led the effort to create the Campaign for High School Equity, a coalition of civil rights organizations dedicated to advancing sound high school reform policies at the federal level. She has also led the development of several key education policy documents; including the Schott Foundation for Public Education's 2020 Vision Roadmap: A Pre-K Through Postsecondary Blueprint for Educational Success and the Campaign for High School Equity's A Plan for Success: Communities of Color Define Policy Priorities for High School Reform.

Dr. Rockeymoore chairs the board of the National Committee to Preserve Social Security and Medicare and serves on the boards of the National Association of Counties Financial Services Corporation, the Campaign for America's Future, and the Economic Policy Institute. She co-chairs the Commission to Modernize Social Security. She is also a member of the National Conference of Black Political Scientists and the Insight Center Experts of Color Network. The recipient of many honors, she was named an Aspen Institute Henry Crown Fellow in 2004 and received Running Start's 2007 Young Women to Watch Award.

Dr. Rockeymoore has been invited to speak before numerous organizations including the Centers for Disease Control and Prevention, Women Donors Network, Grantmakers in Aging, Drexel University, Columbia University, Congressional Democratic Caucus, Congressional Progressive Caucus, and the National Association of Black Journalists among many other groups. She has been quoted in publications such as the New York Times and the Washington Post and has been interviewed on NPR, Sirius XM radio, BET, CNN, and Al Jazeera English among many other media outlets.

Dr. Rockeymoore holds a B.A. in political science and mass communications from Prairie View A&M University and an M.A. and Ph.D. in political science, with an emphasis in public policy, from Purdue University.

# About the Author

A FOURTH-GENERATION WASHINGTONIAN, Angel Rich was raised in a life insurance sales family with a passion for financial literacy. Rich graduated from Hampton University with six honors and studied at the U. of Int'l Business and Economics in Beijing, China. In 2009, Forbes recognized Rich for winning Prudential's national case competition and selling her groundbreaking Generation Y marketing plan.

Becoming a Global Market Research Analyst for Prudential, Rich conducted over 70 financial behavior modification studies including Obama's Veterans Initiative Research Study and the first African American Financial Experience Study. Rich was also recognized with a Presidential Achievement Award for *Exceptional Research and Innovation* for helping Prudential save $6 Billion Rich resigned to found The Wealth Factory in 2013 to design financial literacy edtech games. CreditStacker, her first game, teaches credit management and debt reduction. It is available for free on Google Play and IOS in 40 countries in 4 languages.

The company was named one of the top 10 startups in the world by the State of NY 43North, best financial literacy product in the country by The White House, best learning game by Department of Education, and best solution in the world for reducing poverty from JP Morgan Chase.

Rich has been a featured speaker of the Congressional Black Caucus, Center for Global Policy Solutions, MMTC, SBA, NSBE, Howard University, Hampton University, DC Executive Office of the Mayor, Department of Education, Industrial Bank, MD Cash Campaign, Black Enterprise Entrepreneurship Summit, Walker's Legacy, Google DevFest and more! She has also been featured in several commercials and a PBS NewsHour special.

# Angel Rich

She is the 2015 March of Dimes Rising Heroine of Washington, DC Wells Fargo Spokesperson, Grand Prize winner of Industrial Bank Regional Business Competition and serves on the board of the Charter School Development Corporation. In 2016, Rich was identified as HBCU 30 under 30, Hampton 40 and 40, and one of the top 30 Black Female Founders in the country by Google. By 2017, she became one of the top 4 Black founders in the country by Global 1000 with Jeff Hoffman, Founder of Priceline, calling her "one of his inspirations for waking up in the morning."

Downtown Black Wall Street

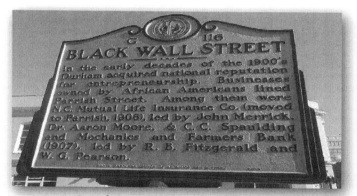

Parrish Street, Durham, North Carolina

Booker T. Washington

The Edmonson Sisters

The Gurley Boarding House

Harriet Tubman

Madam CJ Walker

Rodney Williams

Made in the USA
Middletown, DE
09 July 2023

34744805R00094